TERRA CH

The Global Spiritual Awakening

Ken Carey

This book is manufactured in the United States of
America. Design and cover art by David Burke and
distribution by The Talman Company.

The Talman Company
150 Fifth Avenue
New York, N.Y. 10011

All Scriptural quotations from
authorized King James Version of the Holy Bible

ISBN # 0-912949-02-3

0 9 8 7 6 5 4

A
Uni★Sun
BOOK

To C. S. Lewis

Other books by Ken Carey:

The Starseed Transmissions

Vision

Return of the Bird Tribes

Notes To My Children

TERRA CHRISTA

IV   ATTUNEMENT

V   BIRTH

VI   HEALING

VII   WHOLENESS

VIII   RESURRECTION

PREFACE

Our Creator's purposes appear to be threefold: the enjoyment, the exploration, and the development of space. To further these purposes, the star-system of which we are a part is growing the earth into a sophisticated organ of universal intelligence. The human family is a strategic component of this soon-to-be-completed organism.

Terra Christa invites you to a perspective.

This book looks at Judeo-Christianity in a new way—a way not immune to imperfection, but a way that nevertheless uncovers something meaningful which has been overlooked by our traditions. It represents a lighter, more biological look at the Coming of Christ than perhaps the theologians would prefer, but it is offered in good sport.

I hope that we have emerged into an age when the narrow religious intolerances of the past can be lifted like an unnecessary curfew and laid to rest. We may always have different ways of looking at God. Is that so very bad? The cells of different organs naturally perceive the body from distinct vantage points.

As Christians we do not share a dogma. We share a spirit. Theology has never united us and it never will. Those who dare to take their understanding with a grain of salt discover that behind their differences is a spirit common to all.

This book is a celebration of that Spirit. It speaks of the unparalleled changes that are upon our race and shares experiences, perspectives and principles that can help us better understand them. It speaks of the men and women whose eyes have begun to see the glory of the coming of the Lord. It outlines simple procedures which can make this experience accessible to all. This is not a book about corruption. It fails to mention the Anti-Christ.

This book is about Christ. It tells an abridged tale of humanity's experience with its Creator. It is for anyone who still entertains the prospect of a New Heaven or a New Earth. It is a book for Christians, for Jews, for mainstream church-goers and agnostics alike. It is not recommended for anyone with arthritic understanding, unable to creak into new perspectives. It is a book about life, change, growth, healing, transformation and renewal. It is a book for my friends.

INTRODUCTION

A new generation of Christians is traveling well past the intimidating borders of centuries of tradition to discover the living presence of Christ in their midst. They are becoming aware of a new vision percolating beneath the fabric of their society, seeping through the cracks and crevices of their outworn notions like a great Being waking from centuries of restless slumber.

Already the roots of secular sensibilities are beginning to tremble as this new vision breaks through in bits and pieces. The new physicians at the vanguard of the healing arts are amazed as they discover that healing is an inevitable byproduct of their own love kindling the powers of love in their patients. At the frontiers of science, the new physicists are cataloging the subatomic behavior of playful, creative energies that hint at revolutionary new premises, premises with implications that shake the very foundations of conventional thought. Futurists, historians and sociologists alike all seem to agree that sometime during the next quarter century, the human species will experience a transformation even more fundamental than the shift to an agricultural civilization some ten thousand years ago.

Will this transformation be cataclysmic? Will it be apocalyptic? Or will it be wonderful beyond anything this earth has ever known? I suspect the answers to these questions lie within each one of us. They will vary to the degree that we are each able to align ourselves with the Great Spirit surfacing through our events. If we cling to conceptual interpretations, we are likely to suffer in their inevitable collapse; but if we open our hearts and minds in true humility, to receive again as little children, we are likely to share in the greatest adventure of all time.

What is scripturally encoded in the concise symbolic prose of the Old and New Testaments represents the most remarkable key to human transformation ever compressed into language.

I would like to invite you to join me on a journey of creation and discovery that will lead us deep into the heart of what can only be described as a new world. Partaking of a promise made long ago on the hills of Galilee, we shall travel on the current of the Spirit of truth. We will look at our terrestrial affairs from new eyes. What is occurring among us in the last years of this century marks an end to millennia of darkness. A truly Holy Spirit is waking in the minds and hearts of people the world over, a spirit with a vision, a purpose, a power and a clarity fully capable of helping us see the errors of the past and the possibilities of the present.

Just as the Appalachian Ridge once intimidated the first settlers of the American continent and limited their initial colonization to a narrow coastal band between the mountains and the sea, so contemporary human wisdom, entrenched in a multitude of assumptions and expectations, stretches like an intimidating ridge across the frontiers of what is deemed possible.

If you are one of those who are adventurous enough, bold enough, creative enough, daring enough, to wonder what lies on the other side of this ridge—or if you have already stepped beyond its divide—this book is for you. It is the report of an author and his family who have spent a decade and a half listening in the quietude of the unsettled places: listening to the forests, to the mountains, to the subtle and sometimes distinct voices of nature and nature's God. This report is shared with you as a statement of hope and possibility. It can be done. The new lands are habitable. A spirit of transformation is alive and active in the hearts and minds of a growing number of new pioneers. The ultimate frontier awaits.

I

APPROACH

CLEANSING THE WINDOWS OF PERCEPTION

My nine-year-old son gave me a good lesson once. I had presented him with a Rubic Cube for his birthday, explained its challenge to him and watched as he hopelessly mixed the colors of the cube. We did not have any books that explained how to solve Rubic's challenge, and I did not seriously expect him to sort his way through the billions of possibilities. But one morning as I walked into his room, I had no sooner noticed him sitting on the floor with his cube, when his younger companion suddenly announced, "Fin got his cube fixed!"

A triumphant Fin held up the completed cube. I examined it; sure enough, each of its six sides was once again a solid color. Somewhat incredulous, I asked how he had done it. But before he could explain, his little playmate blurted out, "He switched all the stickers!"

Apparently he had peeled off all 54 of the little colored squares and replaced them on the cube, a solid color on each side. As I thought about this, I realized that his approach showed all the characteristics of true genius.

It seems we often look for the solutions to our problems along linear lines of thought, considering only possibilities which come from anticipated directions. We close ourselves to all kinds of possible solutions that would probably be obvious if we would take our own expectations and belief systems a little less seriously. When we regard our perspective with too much gravity, we bind ourselves to the earth, to a way of looking at things that cannot often see the obvious. The challenge is not to deny or ignore the way we may be viewing things, but to take it lightly, to open ourselves to the possibility that there might be valid perspectives of which we are not aware. G. K. Chesterton once speculated that perhaps the reason the angels could fly was because they took themselves lightly. A lightness of spirit is vital to both perception and understanding.

Like people grouped around a steamed up window arguing about the nature of the blurred shapes and objects that appear outside, our philosophies have attempted to understand human meaning without first cleansing the windows of perception.

Most of us know in our hearts that there is a way we can interact creatively as conscious beings on this planet that is more fun, more enjoyable and more productive. Yet even where this sensing is present, it has traditionally resulted in little more than a periodic and superficial upgrading of belief systems. The challenge, as I see it, is not to improve or modernize the filter through which we observe our world. The challenge is to restore our fundamental trust in life's own inherent intelligence. New and creative ways of seeing things are an inevitable by-product of restored trust in God.

Every one of us shares in the nature of God's genius. It is never too late to open ourselves to an experience of "holy consciousness." The moment we begin taking our fragmented experience lightly, the awareness of our essential wholeness is able to enter. We begin to re-experience ourselves as children of God.

Images born of fragmentation are all that lie between us and true perception. The illusory sense of a fundamentally separate self, intangible as it may seem, lies at the root of our human sorrows. I think children instinctively understand this. I know I did in my pre-school days. I could not begin to articulate it, of course, but I was keenly aware of *everything being one thing*. This is probably why the symbolism of the nursery rhyme, Humpty Dumpty, spoke to me so well.

I was probably no more than two years old when I first learned of Humpty's predicament. When it hit home that this imaginary little creature (who seemed very real to me) was never, no, *never* going to be put back together again, I cried. Later the symbolism became evident.

Humpty represents a whole, integrated and holy universe which has somehow become fragmented at a level where walls divide. "All the King's horses and all the King's men couldn't put Humpty together again." The King symbolizes the separatist consciousness, the ego that usurps the citadel of human decision-making and attempts to rule the land. The horses represent emotional involvement, concerned because the pieces are no longer fitting together as they should. The King's men represent the rational intellect trying to figure out how the pieces might fit in some arbitrary synthesis. It does not occur to any of them to lift their eyes to heaven. They are so busy examining the fragments, they never look to the top of the wall.

While simultaneously lying in pieces at the bottom, Humpty still sits atop the wall. Above the level where walls divide, rests the egg, the sacred circle, the symbol of wholeness and potential.

I cannot help but regard this as excellent news.

HOLY THINKING

Have you ever stood outside surrounded by the stillness of a winter's evening, perhaps in some country place far from the distractions of civilization, and gazed deep into the night sky sparkling with the shining of its myriad stars? Have you ever sensed on such an occasion, woven through all you saw, an intelligence almost too vast to contemplate? On one of those nights when the Milky Way arched across the heavens like a gentle mist of worlds upon worlds, have you felt the genius behind it all, the wisdom sprinkled so generously throughout the stellar order?

I would think it evident that somewhere behind all this precise engineering must lie an intelligence of awesome proportions.

Do you suppose there is some way that the intelligence that coordinates the celestial order might be allowed to coordinate the terrestrial order as well? Suppose this creative intelligence had windows into the human world. Suppose it had a chance to see through human circuitry that did not distort its perceptions. At the very least, problems would be perceived clearly.

One thing is certain: the problems of our global society will not be solved by more of the same kind of fragmented thinking that has created them in the first place. Only a new kind of *holy thinking*, springing from a consciousness of the whole, is likely to introduce the perspectives which will restate humanity's dilemmas in solvable terms. I do not think it is a fuller conceptual picture that we most require, but rather a deeper and fuller experience of ourselves, our world and our

Creator.

Our species is designed to function at the interface of spirit and matter, at the juncture between an eternal Creator and an earthly creation. We are like step-down transformers that translate the creative energies of universal spirit into meaningful activity on earth. But we have allowed reactive behavior to interfere with the proper working of our mental, emotional and physical facilities. Like a short in an electrical circuit, our habitual human behavioral patterns have prevented the finer and more delicate intentions of our Creator from completing their work on earth.

Suppose for a moment that the earth is a single, living organism as many of our ecologists are now suggesting. What healthy organism would be so foolish as to create within itself cells with conflicting purposes and motivations? The fact that human beings *do* often find themselves in conflict with one another indicates that they are out of touch with their own real needs and deeper motivations. Learning to align one's life with the purposes of the Creator introduces a denominator common to all human beings. It makes possible the discovery of individual purposes that are symbiotic and complementary.

THE PURPOSE OF JUDEO-CHRISTIAN TRADITION AND THE WESTERN CULTURE WHICH HAS GROWN UP AROUND IT HAS BEEN TO USHER *HOMO SAPIENS* INTO A SPACE IN CONSCIOUSNESS WHERE THE REMEMBRANCE OF DIVINE PURPOSE CAN OCCUR.

For the individual, divine purpose does not have to be messianic or world-shaking. It is simply a differentiated aspect of the Creator's larger purpose coming to focus in a man or a woman. It could be related to the raising of a family, the development of some new technology, the exploration of possibilities on a musical instrument—there can be an almost infinite number of specific purposes that are all offshoots of the Creator's larger purpose. The miracle of these *healthy* individual purposes is that they never find themselves at odds with the purposes of another who is also in touch with his or her true purpose.

This is a bit of divine magic if you have the eyes to see it.

When human beings are motivated by their true purposes, their outer activities not only do not clash, they actually assist the activities of those around them. What an ingenious way to terminate a conflict-ridden state on earth!

The relationship that a healthy individual has to the wholeness of humankind is like the relationship that a healthy cell in the body has to the body as a whole. There are over 200 different *kinds* of cells in the human body, each with a specific task and purpose in relation to the whole. Differences of perception make it possible for these cells to carry out their various responsibilities. If it were not for a range of perspectives, the body could not function as a single organism. We do not find the adrenals conceiving of themselves as some kind of ethnic minority infringed upon by the adjacent and much larger kidneys. We do not find the circulatory system exploiting the body as some sort of superior commercial civilization sufficient unto itself. The organs and systems of a healthy body work together for the purposes of the whole; this is their fulfillment and joy.

Just as no healthy organism has conflicting cells within itself, no *true* perspectives are ever contradictory. Like spokes on a wheel, they may diverge in a variety of directions, they may embody viewpoints radically distinct, but they all—if we have the honesty to represent them without exaggeration— meet at the hub.

So it is for the human family as we rediscover our true role in the holy biosphere of our Creator. In touch with our long-term purposes and priorities, we find that our individuality complements the individuality of those around us. By serving God's purposes, our own purposes are clarified and fulfilled.

A NEW FUNDAMENTALISM

When Jesus walked the hills of Galilee and taught the human populations of His day, He was not merely presenting a few isolated fragments of truth. He was inviting those to whom He spoke to share in a whole new way of looking at things. He was inviting people to step up into a level of awareness where He and they were one, as He and the Father in Heaven were one. Jesus was not just offering *a* vision, He was offering the Creator's vision. He was extending an invitation to each individual to experience him or herself as a part of a single living being.

Perhaps the first step in accepting such an invitation is to free ourselves from the institutionalized interpretations that have grown up around Christ's teachings. In my own journey toward a new identity in spirit, I know that it has been necessary to relinquish the standard images of what it means to be a Christian. I think this is an important step for each of us. These images cover such a broad spectrum of possible human behavior and are so clouded by the conflicting beliefs of so many Christian sects, there is an initial need to clear the slate. Some of our images may have inherent validity, but, in such cases, they will prove themselves without the necessity of arbitrary maintenance. Others of our images are definite hindrances, having little or nothing to do with true spiritual function.

Why refer to Christianity at all? Why use the Bible as a guide if its language is liable to conjure up inaccurate images?

The Bible is a gift, one that I feel we would be foolish to

ignore. It offers us a language that describes the territory we wish to explore more accurately than any other with which I am familiar. Is the Bible the inspired word of God? Our viewpoints are irrelevant. The Bible is a document of profound significance. Whatever your viewpoint, I invite you to give it a chance; open your heart to it and feel its spirit.

The true follower of Christ follows the current of His living spirit—not the conceptual interpretation of some other human being. This is a vital distinction. It highlights the difference between historical Christianity (which has been largely impotent) and the transformative nature of what we might call "A New Fundamentalism," a fundamentalism that goes back to the true basis of Life: direct personal communion with God. Where such personal communion with God is present, the truth is *experienced* as distinct from the language that describes it.

While the truth might be meaningfully expressed *through* concepts, the truth itself is not a concept; the truth is a living spirit. Concepts can help to clothe this spirit, that it might be comprehensible to the human intellect, but one can get into trouble confusing the clothing with the spirit within. Though the truth may animate a variety of conceptual idioms and be spoken in a thousand languages, it remains nevertheless a living spirit, eternally beyond the clothing that it wears. Remember the commandment?

> Thou shalt not make unto thee any graven image, or any likeness of anything that is in heaven above, or that is in the earth beneath, or that is in the water under the earth. Thou shalt not bow down thyself to them, nor serve them . . .

> Exodus 20: 4 - 5

When I was a child, I skipped over the Second Commandment, dismissing it as inapplicable. I knew I was not about to fashion a golden calf. However, reviewing it later through the eyes of spirit, I was appalled at how straightforward the injunction is here, "Thou shalt not make any graven images."

What is a rigid interpretation of scripture if not a graven image?

We bow down and worship a graven image any time we allow our behavior to be controlled by the extent of our conceptual understanding, rather than by the living spirit of God within. To fashion graven images of the truth and subsequently to allow them to rule our lives is to freeze our level of comprehension and curtail our growth in spirit. It is to cut ourselves off from the moment-by-moment revelation of spirit's organic, living truth and to establish a man-made structure in its place. To create such an image is to create a barrier between ourselves and God. It is to limit our perception to a photograph of reality.

There is nothing inherently wrong, of course, with a concept or a photograph. They are the products of a passing divine panorama. But in right function they are produced *for us* by the overall flow of time and space, and are meaningful only for a limited duration. To latch on to a conceptual snapshot of God or His creation is as foolish as a visitor to England touring the country by train, who takes a photograph of some passing scenery out the train window and then looks at the photograph for the rest of the trip, imagining that she has now "seen" England. She may have seen a fragment of England, but there is considerably more than could ever be captured by a single photograph. Other travelers on perhaps other trains also take their photographs, and they argue with one another as to the nature of England. To possess a collection of graven images of truth is equally foolish. To base our lives on such collections is to disregard the Second Commandment and greatly limit, if not curtail, an ongoing perception of both God and creation.

The truth that *we know* is the truth that we are actually experiencing. To share that living truth through concepts and linguistic descriptions is fine, but to drag such descriptions up out of the past and to let them block a current perception of spirit is to worship false gods.

The age in which we live has worshipped a kind of static understanding that is utterly beside the point in developing true spiritual awareness.

In a culture that places such a high premium on intellectual understanding, it may be useful to study the things of spirit, *but only because the culturally-programmed individual is not likely to otherwise open his or her heart.* There really is no other value in intellectually-gleaned understanding. Genuine understanding of spiritual matters appears in direct proportion to our love. Comprehension is a result of sharing in our Creator's love, a by-product of being connected up to the whole.

To comprehend truth in the absence of love is as impossible as comprehending a telephone message in the absence of electricity. The telephone message rides on the electricity; the truth rides on the current of love.

When we love, we step into a new dimension of perception. Jesus called it the Kingdom of Heaven. Like a channel on another frequency, it waits for us to turn the dial of our attention. When we love, we become conscious of this realm. We come to know the Spirit of truth that inhabits it. We begin to experience some genuine understanding.

THE SPIRIT OF TRUTH

During His years in Galilee, Jesus was sowing the seeds for this generation that is now upon the earth. The new wine of His fuller consciousness could not be poured into the old skins of the men and women who inhabited the lands of the Roman Empire. Jesus pointed to a time in the future when the Spirit of truth would come and guide human beings *into all truth.*

THROUGHOUT THE LONG CENTURIES OF CHRISTIAN CIVILIZATION, THE SPIRIT OF TRUTH HAS BEEN ACTIVELY EDUCATING THE SUBCONSCIOUS OF OUR SPECIES. THERE HAS BEEN A PROFOUND, THOUGH LARGELY UNNOTICED, SHIFT IN THE RESERVOIR OF OUR SUBCONSCIOUS PREDISPOSITIONS.

Thanks in part to the vision of the founding fathers of democracy, who anticipated "a new order of the ages" arising here on North American soil, this continent is currently able to provide an atmosphere highly conducive to the widespread awakening of spirit that has now begun. Before completion, this awakening will affect every member of the global community. So much long range planning has gone into this that it would not be an exaggeration to say that all of history was simply preparation. Countless men and women have lived and died that our generation might now accept the hand that is offered to it and so terminate the long era of darkness that has dominated the earth. At long last, the time has come when the Spirit of truth can consciously begin to surface into the awareness of the new men and women who have been prepared to receive him.

> Howbeit when he, the Spirit of truth, is come,
> he will guide you into all truth: for he shall not
> speak of himself; but whatsoever he shall hear,
> that shall he speak; and he will shew you
> things to come.

John 16: 13

A beautiful picture comes to mind here of the Spirit of truth rising up like a sparkling fountain in the midst of a dry and desolate human island. The bubbling waters of this fountain of truth gradually take on the crystal light form of an angel who reaches out and guides the thirsty human soul *into all truth.* In this metaphorical picture, the dusty island of human experience is surrounded by an ocean of eternal truth. The islanders' custom had been to give lip service to the surrounding ocean, but little else. Occasionally, an individual might make a foray down to the beach, wade out a few feet, take a cupful of the water of truth in his dusty hands and carefully waddle back to the marketplace or the university, the game supposedly being to see who could get the truth farthest inland without it evaporating or spilling.

But this verse indicates that it is not human beings who timidly approach the ocean of truth, get a few facts, gather some data, collect a handful of new information, and then waddle back to their various cultural cisterns to upgrade their quaint belief systems. The image here is of the Spirit of truth, a bubbling fountain of angelic clarity, coming and guiding the individual *into all truth.* Taking the human being by the hand and taking him or her out into the ocean of living information, giving a little push if necessary, telling him or her to go for a swim.

Then for the first time the individual is in a proper relationship with truth, no longer capturing a miniscule fragment of it to further some narrow human purpose, but immersed in it, surrounded by it, supported by it, a part of all truth him or herself. Perhaps such an individual might find that the water is not so cold as imagined, that floating is rather easy once one stops struggling, that swimming actually introduces a refreshing three-dimensional mobility impossible in the shallow cisterns of concept and belief that proliferate on the island.

"But whatsoever he shall *hear,* that shall he speak."

What kind of hearing enables one to receive the Spirit of truth?

> Verily I say unto you, whosoever shall not *receive* the Kingdom of God *as a little child,* he shall not enter therein.

> Mark 10: 15

There is a perceptual openness which enables a child to receive a much broader spectrum of what there is to be perceived than subsequent cultural conditioning allows. A child enters the world equipped for anything, including perception of the Spirit of truth. But then culture draws a box around the child's experience and says, "This is all that is real, all that is permissible, all that is acceptable." The child finds that experience outside the narrow band of the spectrum "approved" by the culture is not communicable. The child also learns that only communicable experience is considered real.

In this way, human cultures have an ingenious method of maintaining taboos; they simply do not provide a language for describing any experience that does not support the dominant fiction.

The developing child is conditioned to ignore a large range of potential input. Without any reinforcement for this whole dimension of experience, the child's perceptual emphasis eventually shifts exclusively over to a culturally accepted range of experience, and the ability to "receive as a little child" atrophies.

The challenge before us is simple: to restore our trust in the Creator who has placed us upon this earth and to *relax* into the currents of His love. As we grow in love and trust, we are once more able to receive as little children. Our ability to hear the Spirit of truth naturally increases and we are shown " . . . things to come."

We gradually become aware of the immense possibilities that open up to human beings who awaken from the subconscious stupor which has characterized the historical era.

WATERS BELOW

The subconscious plays a major role in every imaginable kind of human activity. It is the studio and camera crew behind the theater of terrestrial pageantry, faithfully holding up the stage props of our individual and planetary autonomic processes. It is what keeps every one of our hearts beating and what guides the rhythm of our breath. It digests our food, circulates our blood and periodically recreates our physical bodies. When we sleep at night, it calls us deep into its unfathomable depths and wraps us in its mysteries.

It is appropriate that we are wrapped in mysteries during sleep, but it is not appropriate to remain wrapped in mysteries throughout most of our waking lives.

Humankind has stumbled through a long and painful history wrapped in many unnecessary mysteries. There is nothing to prevent us from de-mystifying ourselves. The subconscious should not dominate the better part of our waking hours.

The subconscious serves several purposes. It provides individual conscious beings with a handy filing system in which to store *the patterns of truth.* When these are activated by *the Spirit of truth,* dimensional expression becomes possible. The subconscious is a realm of memory. It provides continuity with the past. It is also the realm where the basic life-support processes of the physical body are placed on automatic pilot. If it were not for the subconscious mind, the individual would have to devote all of his or her time to keeping the physical body intact. The subconscious is designed to liberate the conscious mind for other activities.

On the planetary scale, the subconscious mind becomes the arena of the great autonomic processes that maintain and balance the myriad systems necessary to the earth's ability to support life. On this level, it can be seen as the subconscious mind of the Creator, containing within it the subconscious mind of each sentient being.

THE DEEPER YOU GO INTO AN INDIVIDUAL'S SUBCONSCIOUS, THE MORE COLLECTIVE IT BECOMES.

At a certain depth, all subconscious minds are joined in the Creator. This is illustrated by the playing board used in the ancient game of Chinese Checkers; six triangles, each with their apex pointing outward, are arranged around a central circular area common to them all. Individual surface consciousness is symbolized by the apex of each triangle. There are only six triangles on the Chinese Checker board, but we can imagine a central circular area surrounded by many triangles, perhaps one for each human being.

As one moves downward, away from the apex of individual consciousness, the triangle grows wider, and one enters the realm of the individual subconscious mind with its childhood memories, etc. As one continues moving further from the apex, the triangle fans out more to include the portion of the subconscious realm shared by the individual's family. Moving down further, ever closer to the central area common to all, the individual comes to a sort of racial or tribal subconscious which is shared with others of similar genetic background. Eventually, he or she emerges into the collective subconscious of *Homo sapiens.*

When the first human beings lost conscious connection with God, the only thing that saved them from physical death was the fact that their subconscious realms were still connected with the Creator's subconscious. Throughout recorded history, this subconscious connection has provided the trickle of life that has sustained humanity. However, it is just a fraction of the energy *Homo sapiens* were designed to run on. Human beings have been like electrical systems which were designed to operate on 120 volts, but which have only been receiving 12. The terminal that connects us to heaven has become corroded with extraneous beliefs and exaggerated fears. We have lost awareness of our collective *supraconscious.*

> And God said, Let there be a firmament in the midst of the waters, and let it divide the waters from the waters. And God made the firmament, and divided the waters which were under the firmament from the waters which were above the firmament: and it was so. And God called the firmament Heaven. And the evening and the morning were the second day.
>
> Genesis 1: 6-8

Figure 1 illustrates the firmament dividing the waters above from the waters below. Many little triangles focus the awareness of the collective subconscious upward, culminating in individual points of human awareness. They are met by corresponding inverted triangles which direct the Creator's consciousness downward.

In the waters above the firmament the Creator has consciousness of Himself as a single being.

The earth is conscious of herself as a single being in the waters below the firmament.

At the horizon where the differentiated aspects of Spirit meet the many focalized essences of matter, humankind is supposed to be conscious of itself as a single being as well. This is the being we refer to as Christ. Christ is the Spirit that is incarnating through the biosphere of the whole earth. His relationship to the earth is similar to the relationship of your spirit to your physical body. We will look at this in more detail later.

In heaven, in the upper range of the firmament, from the horizon of individual human consciousness on up into and through the waters above, Christ is conscious of Himself as a single being. However, humankind does not presently share this consciousness as it was intended to.

Figure 2 shows the range of intended human awareness as opposed to the range of typical historical awareness. Figure 3

FIGURE ONE

WATERS ABOVE

SPIRIT
UNIVERSAL INTELLIGENCE
CHRIST CONSCIOUSNESS

SUPRACONSCIOUS
(REALM OF INTENDED HUMAN FUNCTION)

HORIZON OF INDIVIDUALITY

SUBCONSCIOUS

BOTH
SUBCONSCIOUS
AND
SUPRACONSCIOUS
BECOME
INCREASINGLY
COLLECTIVE AS
THEY MOVE
AWAY FROM THE
HORIZON OF
INDIVIDUALITY

COLLECTIVE UNCONSCIOUS
TERRESTRIAL UNCONSCIOUS

WATERS BELOW

FIRMAMENT
IN THE
MIDST OF
THE WATERS

FIGURE TWO

This illustration is an enlargement of one of the meeting points of subconscious and conscious, represented by the X's in Figure One. It symbolizes something of the vast conscious and subconscious realms that come to a point of differentiated focus in each individual human being and illustrates the intended, as opposed to the typical, range of individual awareness.

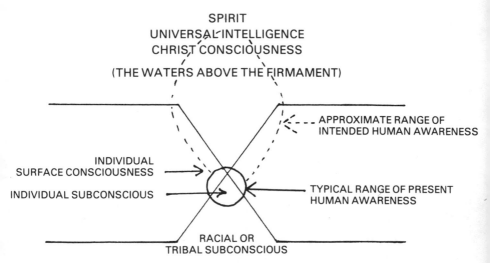

SPIRIT
UNIVERSAL INTELLIGENCE
CHRIST CONSCIOUSNESS

(THE WATERS ABOVE THE FIRMAMENT)

APPROXIMATE RANGE OF
INTENDED HUMAN AWARENESS

INDIVIDUAL
SURFACE CONSCIOUSNESS →

INDIVIDUAL SUBCONSCIOUS

TYPICAL RANGE OF PRESENT
HUMAN AWARENESS

RACIAL OR
TRIBAL SUBCONSCIOUS

(THE WATERS BELOW THE FIRMAMENT)
COLLECTIVE UNCONSCIOUS
SUBCONSCIOUS REALM OF THE EARTH

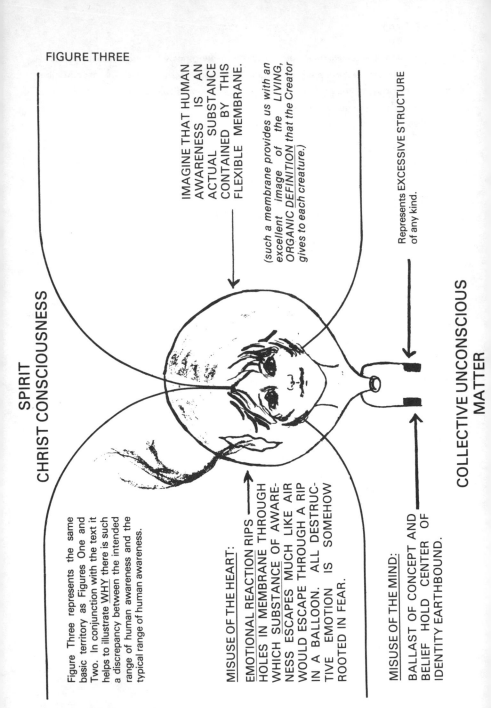

SPIRIT
CHRIST CONSCIOUSNESS

COLLECTIVE UNCONSCIOUS
MATTER

IMAGINE THAT HUMAN AWARENESS IS AN ACTUAL SUBSTANCE CONTAINED BY THIS FLEXIBLE MEMBRANE.

(such a membrane provides us with an excellent image of the LIVING, ORGANIC DEFINITION that the Creator gives to each creature.)

Represents EXCESSIVE STRUCTURE of any kind.

Figure Three represents the same basic territory as Figures One and Two. In conjunction with the text it helps to illustrate WHY there is such a discrepancy between the intended range of human awareness and the typical range of human awareness.

MISUSE OF THE HEART:

EMOTIONAL REACTION RIPS HOLES IN MEMBRANE THROUGH WHICH SUBSTANCE OF AWARE-NESS ESCAPES MUCH LIKE AIR WOULD ESCAPE THROUGH A RIP IN A BALLOON. ALL DESTRUC-TIVE EMOTION IS SOMEHOW ROOTED IN FEAR.

MISUSE OF THE MIND:

BALLAST OF CONCEPT AND BELIEF HOLD CENTER OF IDENTITY EARTHBOUND.

gets into the mechanics of why this is the case.

The extent of individual human awareness is represented by the inflatable membrane in Figure 3. We can think of consciousness as a gaseous substance designed to inflate the membrane until it encompasses the entire range in which the individual is supposed to be aware. There are two reasons why this does not typically take place. The first relates to a misuse of the heart, the second, to a misuse of the mind.

Like an enormous gash in the side of the membrane of human identity, negative emotional reactions allow the precious substance of consciousness to escape. Awareness of the upper realms of spirit diminishes.

On the mental level, the individual's center of identity becomes earthbound. The heavy ballast of concept and belief draws the fallen identity earthward; things appear excessively grave. Self-images emphasize the physical and the external. Belief systems limit understanding and options. Past-oriented structures, graven mental images, are given excessive weight. Assumptions and expectations are unnecessarily heavy. All these things tend to be self-confirming; they guide the individual in and out of experiences that support their fictions. The individual suffers the consequences.

This is our contemporary form of creating and worshipping false gods. It is not all that different from the vicious circles that pagan peoples have often experienced with their deities. It invariably results in disease. There are a couple of simple ways to break out of this syndrome. The first is to become conscious of the fact that it goes on. The second is to relax in the midst of it all and begin to trust in God.

Relaxation allows the emotional realm to settle gently back into a normal, healthy rhythm. It heals the tear in the membrane of identity that was caused by emotional reaction. The substance of consciousness no longer escapes, and the individual's sense of self rises above the momentary confusion. The individual re-enters the realms of consciousness where he or she belongs.

OUTRUNNING DEPRESSION

During my early 20's I went through a dark period of several months. I was extremely depressed. I had recently lost both my parents. I was out of work and money. I had a family to support. I was dealing with the kinds of things that most people deal with sometime or other. But I was not dealing with them well. I was getting caught in a vicious circle. I was unable to sleep at night, which lowered my resistance. Consequently I became sick and found myself worrying more, sometimes staying awake all night. And on and on it went. I was probably well on the way to what could have been more serious problems, when suddenly I realized that I was afraid. This was actually a welcome realization. Fear was something tangible, something I felt I could deal with.

Depression had been a vague looming shadow across my whole outlook. It seemed rooted in so many nebulous intangibles, I had never been able to get my hands on it. One day it struck me, however, that all depression was rooted some way or another in anxiety. I knew that anxiety was just fear dressed up to look respectable. So I acknowledged the basic survival fears that had been lurking behind my anxiety. When I honestly appraised my situation, I saw that my survival fears were greatly exaggerated. My situation was not *that* bad! I was afraid of *my description* of reality.

I went back in my imagination to the tropical savannah grass and imagined myself confronting a tiger. Fight/flight instincts were triggered; my body prepared to either fight or run. I became extremely awake and alert (insomnia). My bowels prepared themselves for flight (constipation). Fear (disguising itself first as anxiety and then as depression) had prepared my body to run. Yet I had been lying sick and sleepless in bed for days. I made an instant decision. I overrode the objections of my logic. I felt my life depended on the radical course of action that had intuitively come to mind.

I climbed out of my sickbed and shakily tied on my running shoes. "So you're prepared to run are you, body?" I walked outside onto the dirt road that ended at our forest home. I imagined that my anxiety-ridden description of reality and my survival fears were objectified in the form of a great tiger. I shot one glance at it and took off running down the road as if my life depended upon it. Who knows? Perhaps at that point it did.

My logic and reason were telling me I was going to make myself seriously ill. They argued that I was out of shape, that I hadn't eaten or slept properly in weeks, that I obviously had some kind of virus.

I left them behind after a few hundred yards.

The great depression tiger fell behind as I approached the quarter-mile mark (apparently he was out of shape too — the spirit of depression isn't often required to hustle to keep up with a host).

Fluttering around me like horseflies, the little whispers of anxiety did their best to keep up. I ran for all I was worth. At the half-mile mark they too began to drop back. I was winning the race. Suddenly I began feeling like the twenty-some-odd-year-old athelete that I was. An indescribable joy flooded my heart. I felt euphoric. I decided to run all the way to our mailbox a full mile away. I was both laughing and crying as I ran back home.

I slowed to a walk as I approached the house. What a wonderful discovery! During my run I had seen clearly that depression is not able to establish a foothold unless fear of some sort is present. Walking back into the yard, I felt so good, so whole, so filled with joy, such a strong momentum of healing taking place around and within me, that I decided to pursue the subject and see if I might be able to pinpoint a sort of primal fear.

My intuition had won a victory. The run it had suggested had been a success. It must have known its credibility was up, for it seemed to be pressing its advantage. It was telling me that there is an archetypal fear behind all fear.

I sat down on the front steps and used my newfound sense of energy to look at myself. Possibly it was because I had recently been sick, possibly it was because the run had done something strange to my body chemistry. In any event, I had the distinct impression of going deep within. I closed my eyes and could almost feel my ancestors surrounding me. I went deeper and began to experience myself as a much larger being, an eternal being. I came very close to a sort of veil, an interface where my individuality began to blur into God's wholeness. I felt love like I had never felt it before; I felt as if I were suspended in an ocean of love. God how I loved! How I loved God! It was so glorious to be near Him, to be in His presence. *Being* seemed to ripple through the air around me.

If loving God had been wonderful, feeling God's love was beyond all superlatives. I felt His love become increasingly specific as it approached me from the center of His being, from the center of all being. It seemed to crackle in the air around me like some multi-colored electrical network. I felt God loving me into being. I felt His love defining me in His image and likeness.

A long period of time elapsed. I have no real way of knowing how long it might have been. I seemed to float effortlessly in an ocean of eternal being. I was aware of myself as being distinct from God but only in the dreamy way a fish must feel distinct from the ocean. Whatever I was, was made out of God. God was inside me, all around me.

After a long while I felt myself gently drift up against the edge of something. I recognized it as Time and Space. I slowly began to drift through it, as if it were a kind of veil in the ocean of eternal being. All around me I watched as the most exquisite and elaborate geometric shapes took form. I realized that my own essence was becoming objectified; my talents, my qualities, my interests were forming into living structures that grew and expanded and changed before my eyes. It seems I was just beginning to recognize some of the geometric patterns as cells, organs and systems in a slowly developing body, when I had a curious thought. It went something like this:

"It is so wonderful to be a part of God, it feels so good to feel my roots deep in His being. How I hope it all goes on and on; it would certainly be terrible if suddenly God were not here."

The rest happened in a flash. I must have nodded off, for I suddenly jerked my head up and found myself sitting on the front steps. The last sensation I remember before opening my eyes had been a sense of falling. It probably coincided with my head dropping forward just before I awoke.

"So this is what lies at the root of all fear!" I realized it as distinctly as if it had been engraved in stone: *Behind all fear is the thought of separation from God.*

That evening I ate a hearty meal and followed it with the first good night's sleep I'd had in months. In a couple of days I was back to normal. I found a job. The details of my life fell into place.

HEALING THE ONLY ENEMY

Human attention is charged with the ability to create. When human attention is focused on negative emotions, those negative emotions take on a quasi-life of their own. Consequently, there are whole families of ill spirits: spirits of greed, spirits of resentment, spirits of shame, spirits of blame, hate, fear, anger and so forth. We call them by a score of names, but they are all hapless creatures of human ignorance. They are born through the misuse of human creativity. They have no life apart from the life that unconscious human beings foolishly channel into them.

Our collective subconscious is teeming with such ill spirits. Like dark gray clouds, they drift through the lower part of the firmament. They have an elementary form of self-awareness. On the surface they crave the energy they receive when human beings identify with them and express them; but that is only what *they think* they want. What they really want, what they long for, is to be free. Their only exit point is through the conscious minds of human beings. Bringing them into full consciousness is the first step toward their dissolution.

The times when we are feeling emotional turbulence are our most profound opportunities to cast out ill spirits. These times are not pleasant, but they *are* essential. If we do all that we can to avoid ever feeling emotional discomfort, we refuse to participate in healing these ill spirits. And as long as they remain within us, subliminally influencing our awareness, we never awaken. We do not need to seek out emotional encounters, but when they come our way in the natural ebb and flow of life, we should appreciate the fact that these times have every bit as much value as our more enjoyable "peak experiences."

Whenever I feel the presence of an ill spirit, I know I have a tremendous opportunity, an opportunity to offer a healing deep into the collectivity of my race. As I feel the ill spirit creeping up on me, I take a moment or two to bring it into full consciousness. I find it helpful to be right out front and to say to myself, "*OK, what exactly am I afraid of?*" It is important not to be fooled by the clever disguises that fear can take. "I'm not afraid, I'm angry," the mind will often try to argue. Yes, but an honest examination will invariably show that the anger is rooted in some sort of fear. So, of course, is resentment and shame and greed. Sometimes the connection with fear takes detective work to uncover, but the principle holds true: every ill spirit is rooted in fear. Its antidote is love.

Jesus taught that we should love our enemies. Who are our *real* enemies? Enemies of happiness? Enemies of creativity? Enemies of joy and peace?

SPIRITS SUCH AS ANGER, RESENTMENT, GUILT AND ANXIETY ARE OUR REAL ENEMIES. THEY ARE PARASITES THAT FEED UPON HUMAN CONSCIOUSNESS.

In their primitive level of self-awareness, ill spirits are far from happy. They long to be freed. No one, on any occasion, has ever loved them. They do not know what love is; yet they instinctively grope for it. They crave the love that alone can free them. The illustrations in figures 4-A and 4-B show how ill spirits are typically treated. They are usually either *expressed* or *repressed.* Both approaches give them huge injections of human energy. Both expression and repression drain the individual psychologically and emotionally, and both leave the ill spirit recharged, looking for another opportunity to be acknowledged and fed.

Figure 4-C illustrates the approach of the healer. It is quite different from the first two. We do not repress the ill feeling, pretend it is not there, or gloss over it with feigned spirituality. But neither do we identify with the reactive emotion and claim

FIGURE FOUR

DEALING WITH "ILL SPIRITS"

A.

WATERS ABOVE
_____

FIRMAMENT

REPRESSION

WATERS BELOW

This is a short-term approach. It dissipates much human energy and can lead to eventual illness.

B.

WATERS ABOVE
_____

FIRMAMENT
HARMFUL
BEHAVIOR ← HUMAN ENERGY

EXPRESSION

WATERS BELOW

This approach often leaves you exhausted and simply leaves the ill spirit "recharged" for its next attack.

C.

WATERS ABOVE
_____

FIRMAMENT

HEALING

WATERS BELOW   STEP ONE   STEP TWO

This approach offers a profound healing into the collective sub-conscious.

"But I say unto you . . . Love your enemies"

it as our own. We do not get all worked up and tell so-and-so exactly how we feel or go looking for someone to hear our complaints.

We may be trembling from head to toe, but we hold steady. We acknowledge the presence of the alien. We let ourselves experience it fully. We take a couple of deep breaths and let it flood our being. We meet it consciously with the spirit of welcome. We invite it up out of the subconscious realm into the conscious realm that it has instinctively longed for since it was first created. As we continue breathing deeply, we feel it permeate our entire body; as it seems to flood our circuitry, we bring it all the way up into our full conscious attention, and *we let our love radiate*. We remember our Creator. We experience the love that is the birthright of all conscious beings. The ill spirit dissolves. Its energy is released. It is evaporated in heaven.

Ill spirits are nothing anyway, bubbles of nothing in an ocean of consciousness. Only the surface energy which they trap has any reality. Inside they are empty. In one form or another they embody the absence of love. As we allow the spirit of love to be expressed through us, love fills every void we encounter. We dissipate the ghosts of past human ignorance. We heal the only enemy.

II

GENESIS

THE MARRIAGE OF STAR AND STONE

The Creator's understanding is available to us in every moment. But it is such a jump from the typical manner of subjective human thought, that without some intermediate conceptual bridging, it would be difficult for most of us to span the chasm. To be meaningful, the transition from the known into the unknown requires reference points in the familiar. Yet even these reference points should be taken with a grain of salt.

The perspectives that I am about to share should not be taken as absolute statements of truth. They are merely conceptual triggers with the capacity to release a deeper, experiential understanding in some people. They are tools that might help to adjust the rhythms of our individual understanding so that they might correlate with the ongoing comprehension of the Creator.

The Genesis account of Creation and the subsequent Fall refers to more than just the early days of humanity. It is a multi-leveled narrative that can also be seen as the story of the creation and fall of each individual human being. It is the story of our inability to remain consciously within the creative field that is sustained through the relationship of spirit and matter. The first three chapters of Genesis outline creative conditions which have never changed. Each verse in these chapters is like the tip of an iceberg with dimensions of meaning resting unseen behind the specific words. The first chapter describes the ground rules for the sustenance of a physical sphere of creative interaction.

> 1 In the beginning God created the heaven and
> the earth.
> 2 And the earth was without form, and void;
> and darkness was upon the face of the deep.
> And the Spirit of God moved upon the face of
> the waters.

Genesis 1: 1-2

It is significant to note the sequence: God created the *heaven* and *then* the *earth*. The heaven was created first.

WHAT MANIFESTS ON EARTH IS ALWAYS A RESULT OF PRIOR CREATIVE INTENT IN HEAVEN.

Behind all manifest physical phenomena is an invisible realm of design where pure form exists in essence. Today's physicists refer to this realm as "a substrata of primal vibrational patterning." Jesus simply called it the Kingdom of Heaven. It is here in this level of pre-form that the Creator initially established the perfect design for each and every living creature. In the chapter entitled *Healing In Heaven*, we will explore this further. For now, let us move on and get the general picture.

> 3 And God said, Let there be light: and there
> was light.
> 4 And God saw the light, that it was good; and
> God divided the light from the darkness.
> 5 And God called the light Day, and the
> darkness he called Night. And the evening and
> the morning were the first day.
> 6 And God said, Let there be a firmament in
> the midst of the waters, and let it divide the
> waters from the waters.
> 7 And God made the firmament, and divided
> the waters which were under the firmament
> from the waters which were above the fir-
> mament: and it was so.
> 8 And God called the firmament Heaven. And
> the evening and the morning were the second
> day.

Genesis 1: 3-8

The earth began to experience the activity of the sun on the face of her waters, temperatures moderated, and the waters of the largely oceanic planet released an atmosphere, a firmament in the midst of them, conducive to life. The atmosphere of the earth marked the surface where starlight and (star) matter were to interact. It was here at the interface between spirit and matter that a biosphere was to be born. It was here that a balanced blending could take place between star and stone, physically and spiritually.

The firmament in the midst of the waters separated the conscious and the subconscious, allowing God's creativity to interact with the earth through two distinct natures. Some of the processes through which things came into form were left conscious while others were made subconscious. The firmament divides the aspects of creation which require conscious attention from those which do not. This arrangement freed up the Creator to function within a landscape of autonomic processes. It enabled Him to spend time on detail.

> 9   And God said, Let the waters under the heaven be gathered together unto one place, and let the dry land appear: and it was so.
> 10 And God called the dry land Earth: and the gathering together of the waters called he Seas: and God saw that it was good.
> 11 And God said, Let the earth bring forth grass, the herb yielding seed, and the fruit tree yielding fruit after his kind, whose seed is in itself, upon the earth: and it was so.
> 12 And the earth brought forth grass, and herb yielding seed after his kind, and the tree yielding fruit, whose seed was in itself, after his kind: and God saw that it was good.
> 13 And the evening and the morning were the third day.
>
> Genesis 1: 9-17

These verses pertain to planetary autonomic processes that were set in motion at this time. These processes were "gathered together into one place," that is, they were motivated by a single creative intention, for a single creative purpose. These six verses tell the abridged story of the creation of the basic life-support systems which set the stage for later animal and human life. It was at this stage that the Creator established the mechanisms that would regulate the amount of gasses in the atmosphere, the overall temperatures of the planet, the nature of its vegetation, etc.

The environmental support systems which undergird conscious human life are governed and maintained by these "waters under the Heaven." What was initiated here and set in motion was intended to be left alone. It did not require conscious monitoring or interference. It provided a context for future creation, the canvas, so to speak, on which the divine artist would subsequently paint. This third creative day correlates with the Earth cycle, things taking form. The principle of seeds unfolding into the objectification of specific potentialities was here established. "And the evening and the morning were the third day."

GOD SEEDS

Now we move on to the fourth creative day, when the far more intense energies of God's love could at last begin to multiply in the context of a creative field designed to provide them with maximum support.

> 14 And God said, Let there be lights in the firmament of the heaven to divide the day from the night; and let them be for signs, and for seasons, and for days and years:
> 15 And let them be for lights in the firmament of the heaven *to give light upon the earth*: and it was so.
>
> Genesis 1: 14-15

THE FIRMAMENT IN THE MIDST OF THE WATERS THAT GOD CALLED HEAVEN IS THE FREQUENCY RANGE ON WHICH HUMAN BEINGS WERE DESIGNED TO FUNCTION.

Within its range (which correlates physically with the atmosphere of the earth) differentiated aspects of God's spirit were to clothe themselves in material bodies and grow, in oneness with those bodies, into ever expanding universal awareness.

Taking place simultaneously was the education and awakening of the earth itself. Through the development of biological forms of life culminating in human beings, the Creator was drawing forth the immense potential of the planet. The earth was growing organs of perception far beyond what she had developed as an inorganic satellite of the sun, emerging into a level of conscious life previously only experienced by stars. But this was not the whole of the process.

WHILE HUMANKIND WAS DEVELOPING INTO A KIND OF CENTRAL NERVOUS SYSTEM FOR THE PLANET, TINY SEEDS OF GOD'S IDENTITY WERE TO BE SPROUTING THROUGH THE INDIVIDUAL HUMANS INVOLVED.

Though not all of them would take full advantage of it, the opportunity was present for each of these *God-seeds* to reach a level of spiritual maturity wherein they might come to know their Creator as a friend and partner. The 14th and 15th verses of the first chapter of Genesis depict the Creator taking a part of His very being and allowing it to differentiate as *lights* (plural) in the firmament of heaven.

Seeds are planted on the fourth day. Conscious entities, the essential spirits of human-beings-to-be, are created *in heaven.* They did not have physical bodies at this point. They were placed initially in their primary element, the air of spirit, as lights of intelligence. Their function was to divide the day from the night, to clearly distinguish the conscious realms from the subconscious. "And let these be for signs, for seasons, for days and for years."

A sign is a symbol, the distilled essence of a greater truth. These spiritual precursors of physical human beings were distilled essences of divine qualities and characteristics. They were to exist for seasons, for days and for years. They were like God Himself, in His image and likeness. They possessed a quality of duration. Their purpose was to give light *upon the earth.* They were to be the physical representatives of God's conscious intelligence *within creation.*

Each was a fragment of God's light, destined to become a cell in His terrestrial body, designed to grow and shed the light of intelligence upon the earth. These would eventually form the species that would allow matter to awaken to a much greater awareness of herself, the species that would allow Christ to incarnate.

Christ is that aspect of the Creator which enters into conscious relationship with creation. Christ was one with the Creator throughout all the events recorded in Genesis.

The 20th through 26th verses of the first chapter of Genesis now describe how God began to invest differentiated aspects of His identity in temporal, material form. All of the animal species created between the time lights were placed in the heavens and the creation of physical man (the 26th verse) can be seen as objectifications of *subconscious* aspects of humanity itself. Since one of the functions of humanity was to provide an organ of self-consciousness for the earth, animal and vegetable kingdoms are contained within the framework of humanity's true definition.

"And God said, let us make man in our image, after our likeness; and let them have dominion . . . "

THE FIRST HUMAN PHYSICAL BODIES WERE MINIATURE SYMBOLIC MODELS OF THE EARTH'S NATURE AND THE CREATOR'S NATURE COMBINED.

Their inhabitants were to enter a training period that would bring them through a joyful age of partnership with matter, ever drawing it upward into expanded awareness. Through this process, matter was to be taught immortality. Matter was to learn to develop an identity that was not contingent upon any specific form expanding its sense of self into the mental and spiritual. As long as its sense of self was contingent upon specific structure, matter's spiritual life-span was finite.

Through human beings, the soul of matter, the essence of their mother planet, was to be taught a spiritual existence on the finer vibrational frequencies of light, sound and energy. Humankind would provide other services as well, but one of its secondary roles was to teach the earth the language of light.

The primary human role was to consciously guide the potentialities of eternal spirit into tangible, three-dimensional form. Through *Homo sapiens,* the Creator could experience previously invisible aspects of His intelligence as objectified biological structure. These new creatures provided a way for God to share His existential pleasure.

HISTORICAL GESTATION

You can imagine an artist's delight at bringing into existence a whole new kind of substance, substance at once both matter and energy, light and stone. Biological life represented a unique medium through which a new kind of art could emerge. Vast dimensions of universal potentiality could be brought into form through the biological blending of earth and sun, possibilities denied either star or stone alone.

Of all these possibilities, humankind was the most exciting. Through this species, balanced at the precise midpoint between spirit and matter, the Creator would one day consciously enter His own creation and for the first time in all history explore the creative miracles that might take place when He was dressed in a physical family. Each individual god-being in this family would, when a sort of collective gestation process was complete, share in the totality of God's perceptions, as well as in the subjectivity of his or her environmental moment. Identity would oscillate back and forth, ebbing and flowing, between the whole and the part, as it does between the consciousness of any healthy organism and its individual cells.

Before the Fall caused the age of gestation to stumble into recorded history, God gave human beings dominion over the earth, a kind of shared stewardship for the planet and for the forms of lesser intelligence that were developing upon it. Before they were to awaken, at the end of the gestation period, into awareness of themselves as god-beings functioning together in a single family-like organism, human beings were to enjoy a period of stewardship as conscious individual god-beings blending the wisdom of an awakening earth with the wisdom of the Creator. During this period, creative activity on earth would be guided and directed with greater precision than ever before.

Human beings were to be like the delicate paint brushes that the artist uses to indicate the subtle detail of a painting, after the cruder, more general aspects of the landscape have been arranged.

> And the Lord God planted a garden *eastward*
> in Eden: and there he put the man whom he
> had formed.
>
> Genesis 2: 8

The Creator cultivated a specific climate upon the earth in which human beings could flourish. The garden was oriented *to the east*, to the direction from which the sun rises, to the point on the horizon where the source of terrestrial energy appears each day. The individual human body, with its autonomic processes, was also facing the source of life. It was oriented towards God's will, toward the life-giving options coming out of God's presence. The earth garden and the individual body garden were both functioning at this time as they were designed to function; their polarity was in spirit.

THE POLAR SHIFT

We speak of the earth possessing a quality of polarity; it has a magnetic field with a north pole and a south pole. We seldom think of the individual human being as possessing a similar quality of polarity. Yet the principle is as valid on the individual level as it is on the planetary.

Scientists will occasionally refer to a time in the past when the earth's poles are said to have shifted. Apparently this is suggested by the remains of tropical animals and vegetation found frozen deep beneath the arctic ice. It would not be surprising to learn some day that the shifting of the earth's poles coincided with a shift in the polarity of the first humans.

Human beings were created to inhabit the mid-range of the firmament of Heaven. They were designed to function at the balance point between an eternal spirit and a material planet. Their home was a domain of precise balances. They were the embodiments of the focalized essences of all the constituents they were balancing. Their physiology was symbolic; it correlated with the animal, vegetable and mineral kingdoms over which they were to provide stewardship. Their spiritual natures were also symbolic. They brought the vast realms of consciousness into specific attitudes, characteristics and focal points of awareness. *But their polarity was in spirit.* They were oriented to their source in the Creator.

The theory of evolution can be misleading; it looks at the emergence of *Homo sapiens* upside down. It presupposes a human polarity in the earth. The first humans had no such polarity. They had their polarity in spirit. They took their identity, their sense of who they were, from the spirit which had incarnated. They were created in the image and likeness of God. Their physical bodies had been formed while they were in conscious communion with the Spirit of God, shaped and molded from the dust of the ground by the Creator Himself. Of course, the matter in which they were being clothed was experiencing something too; there was a certain earthly nature present which could well have seen itself as evolving. But the earth nature was designed to be a secondary, subconscious component of identity. It was intended to be subservient to spirit until the end of the collective gestation. Human beings were not created to receive their direction from the evolving identity of their mother planet. They were to receive their direction from the Creator.

In the beginning, the awakening consciousness of the earth could not comprehend spirit directly. She needed tangible intermediaries. Humankind was the earth's most practical and immediate representative of spirit. Human beings provided objectified, three-dimensional spirit in a form that the earth could observe closely. Under the direction of spirit, the first humans taught the earth the ways of spirit. They used dramatizations of water, air, earth, and particularly fire. They portrayed the nature of spirit as analogous to the sun. The awakening earth could understand this.

When the Fall occurred, human polarity suddenly shifted. The effects on the planet were profound. Suddenly human beings were looking to their environment for direction. The earth found herself confronting a fearful race of creatures whom she could no longer trust. The earth used her subconscious influence to teach the fallen humans to orient toward spirit, to orient toward her symbol of spirit, the sun. From this a primitive form of sun worship was born; but it was inevitably distorted. No mere symbol, however bright and glorious, could yet restore humanity's conscious connection with God. The polarity reversal thoroughly altered the relationship between human beings and the earth. It also put an end to conscious communications between Creator and creation.

A CURIOUS THING HAPPENS WHEN POLARITY IS

REVERSED; THAT WHICH ONCE ATTRACTED
REPELS, AND THAT WHICH ONCE REPELLED
ATTRACTS.

This can be demonstrated with three little donut shaped
magnets (figure 5). Use the lower magnet to represent the
earth. Place it on a pencil with its negative pole facing upward.
Place a second magnet on the pencil representing human
beings. As in figure 5-A, portray these human beings in
healthy polarity. They represent the Creator to the earth, so
their positive pole is downward. In this polarity, they are immediately drawn into a close symbiotic working relationship
with the mother planet. The third magnet represents the
Creator whose positive pole is facing downward. Since
humankind has its negative pole facing upward as it represents
the earth to the Creator, human beings are immediately drawn
into a conscious working relationship with the Creator. All
three magnets now sit on the pencil as close to one another as
possible.

Now notice what occurs (figure 5-B) when human polarity is
reversed: suddenly humankind's positive pole is facing the
Creator's positive and the two positives repel; its negative pole
is facing the earth's negative and the two negatives repel. All
three magnets hang suspended on the pencil as far apart as the
strength of their charges permit.

We can understand why the human polarity reversal
benefits neither earth nor Creator; *it effectively sabotages the
conscious range of their spirit/matter relationship.* It draws
the conscious range of their relationship deep into the subconscious realm. Before we had written histories, the old story-
tellers would refer to this as "the time when the fathers fell
asleep." This is precisely what occurred.

The creative process was designed to draw out the earth's
potential. It was to lift matter up into the designs of spirit,
exploring all the possibilities of clothing spirit with matter.
The Divine Design radiated initially through the Creator's
positive intention. It was *received* by healthy humans with
their orientation (their receptive face) toward God. The
Creator's intention was then translated by the human beings

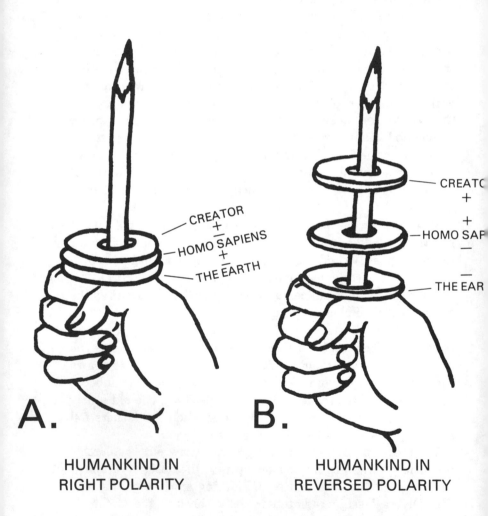

FIGURE FIVE: Magnets on pencils demonstrate the effect of a reversal in human polarity.

CREATOR
+
HOMO SAPIENS
+
THE EARTH

CREATO
+
+
HOMO SAP
−
−
THE EAR

A.

B.

HUMANKIND IN
RIGHT POLARITY

HUMANKIND IN
REVERSED POLARITY

into a range of specific activities. These activities interacted *positively* with the earth, drawing forth her potential.

Before the Fall, human needs were met through the same kind of symbiosis that occurs within the bodies of all healthy organisms. Just as the blood delivers oxygen to the cells of the body, so human physical needs were met easily, without "sweat of the face." When human polarity reversed, people found themselves afraid of both God and the earth. They found that their level of consciousness now repelled the very things that they needed for survival.

It is important to realize that the Fall occurred only on the conscious levels of human function. It could not have occurred on subconscious levels, because humans had no free will in this autonomic realm. Except for a thin film on the surface, which is distorted by ill spirits, humankind's subconscious has remained healthy.

Because humankind's subconscious *is* in right polarity, we experience a *relatively* healthy biosphere. The areas where the biosphere is unhealthy are the areas where fallen human activities have distorted the life-processes involved. Because humankind was designed to represent the earth to the Creator and because human physiology is *homologous* (analogous in a biological way) to the animal, vegetable and mineral kingdoms, there is not one of these kingdoms that has not in some way been negatively influenced by the reversal of conscious human polarity. This negative influence has been very little on the mineral kingdom, only slightly felt in the vegetable kingdom, but it has been significant—almost disastrous—in the animal kingdom. This is not the place to go into this in depth. I mention it in this context to remind those who would look to nature for models of health, that nature herself has been distorted by the reversal of conscious human polarity. The human observer affects all that is observed.

To the extent that we are consciously able to see where we first went wrong, we begin to reverse the process. This would be impossible alone, of course, but there is a powerful momentum of healing that we will find helping us as we go along. Spirit has not been idle all these millennia.

Since *conscious* communication with *Homo sapiens* became extremely difficult after the Fall, God began, at that time, to devote His energies to the process of educating humankind's collective subconscious. Shortly after the first humans fell under the deceptive spell of good and evil, the creator planted within humankind the seeds that would grow into eventual awakening, polarity reversal and healing. These seeds broke through on a conscious level in Galilee, when Christ's planetary-wide awareness was articulated on earth for the first time since the Fall. When, at the conclusion of His time on earth, Jesus said, "I go unto the Father to prepare a place for you," He was referring to His activities during the final two millennia of this many millennia-long period of subconscious education.

Jesus knew that His activities in the collective subconscious would one day culminate with His awareness bubbling under the surface of every man, woman and child on the face of the earth.

Though we find ourselves today with a certain cultural, historical crust that remains to be broken through, the good news is that we have the irresistible momentum of thousands of years of subconscious education on our side. Millennia-old habits do not necessarily have to die hard.

MIND/BRAIN IN THE MIDST OF THE GARDEN

The Fall could not have occurred as a collective historical event if it had not first occurred on the level of the individual. The Fall was a personal event, with personal implications.

While the garden depicted in the Genesis account of the Fall can be seen as a geographical location, it can also be seen as one's most immediate physical domain: one's physical body. There are other levels of interpretation that are equally valid, but it may be useful this once to pursue the thread of a personal interpretation through the events that follow.

If the garden (in which the man was put) is seen as a physical body, then the tree planted in the midst of the garden can be seen as the body's central nervous system. The uppermost and primary part of the central nervous system is the human mind/brain. It is the mind/brain (and its attendant network of sensors) which enables the individual human being to see, smell, hear, taste and feel. It is the mechanism that allows perception of the material world on its own terms. It is also what permits the individual to reflect the universal nature of deity in spatial and temporal form.

THE HUMAN MIND/BRAIN IS THE MOST EXQUISITE OF OUR PHYSICAL SYSTEMS, WITH CIRCUITRY INTERWOVEN THROUGHOUT THE BODY, IN APPEARANCE NOT UNLIKE A TREE, ITS ROOT SYSTEM AND BRANCHES.

This mind/brain tree that is planted in the center of the body garden is pleasant to the sight; indeed, it makes sight and all other sensations possible. It is good for food; it is the means by which the individual obtains the physical necessities of survival. It is also the tree of the knowledge of good and evil. Yes, the same tree, used in a different capacity, would provide the newly incarnate human creatures with the knowledge of good and evil. But use of this tree in that capacity was not to be activated for quite some time yet—not until the human family had multiplied and filled the earth, not until a whole yet-to-be age of individual experience in the garden had come to pass.

> And the Lord God took the man and put him into the garden of Eden to dress it and to keep it.
>
> Genesis 2: 15

One of the purposes that human beings were to serve in the Garden was to preside as stewards over the matter that was continuously flowing in and out of their bodies, that this matter might be held suspended in the designs of God's spirit. They were to dress their spiritual bodies in matter and keep them in manifestation.

Even in today's scientific era, people often forget that the cells in their bodies are continuously being created anew. Matter is literally flowing into and out of their bodies all the time. In the course of a lifespan of seventy years, many bodies come and go.

Then why is scar tissue reproduced? Why do organs deteriorate? Why is there aging and death?

> And the Lord God commanded the man, saying, Of every tree of the garden thou mayest freely eat: But of the tree of the knowledge of good and evil, thou shalt not eat of it: for in the day that thou eatest thereof thou shalt surely die.
>
> Genesis 2: 16-17

The mind/brain and its attendant network of sensors can be used in a variety of ways. There are many aspects of the tree planted in the midst of the garden. But to use this tree *to sub-jectively evaluate good and evil* was forbidden the newly in-carnate humans. To ignore this vital instruction would be to jeopardize their residency in the garden. "For in the day that thou eatest thereof thou shalt surely die."

The Fourth Commandment as recorded in Exodus 20: 12 also touches on this: "Honour thy father and thy mother: that thy days may be long upon the land which the Lord thy God giveth thee."

The first land given to each human being is the land of his or her physical body. If the soul's residency in that land is to be long, there is the necessity of honoring one's father and one's mother. There is certainly wisdom in honoring one's genetic parents, but that is not the primary message here. Who are the soul's true parents? The earth is the Mother, the Creator, the Father. The human being who would enjoy a long life must honor *both* parents. The Creator is honored by a welcome readiness to obey. The earth is honored by the activities of benevolent stewardship.

The Creator knew that certain materialistic tendencies would accompany the incarnation of His human spirits. To forcibly repress or eliminate these would have been to remove the raw material which was being refined through the con-sciousness of the awakening earth. It would have also removed human volition and thoroughly altered the fun-damental nature of humankind. No, these earthly tendencies had to remain, but their "common sense" was not to have had free reign; it was to have been complemented by a deeper sense that would instruct it in the ways of spirit. The two superim-posed natures were to build upon one another's strengths.

> And the Lord God commanded the man, saying, Of every tree of the garden thou mayest freely eat: But of the tree of the knowledge of good and evil, thou shalt not eat of it . . . . "
>
> Genesis 2: 16-17

All trees have a commonality of principle, whether an oak, a pine, a beach or a maple; a tree has a *treeness* about it, a certain tree nature. There were a number of ways this one tree in the midst of the human body could manifest, a wide range of "fruit" available from its branches. But decisions which sprang from its subjective knowledge of good and evil were forbidden. Motivation was to come from spirit.

Motivation was to shine from the center of God's creative intentions like a great light that would then be differentiated into a thousand sub-purposes through the prism of humankind.

Humankind was not to have shared in the generation of purpose until it had come to a greater understanding of the nature of the terrestrial panorama and its own roots in eternal spirit. If questions of good and evil were taken into the hands of these highly subjective human creatures too soon, a fatal feedback could result which would greatly limit the amount of time an individual soul could stay in a physical body. Such an eventuality would not likely terminate the period of humanity's gestation, but it would definitely make the process less enjoyable for the individuals involved. The newly created identity shimmering in the branches of the tree in the center of the garden was to have had a training period, stewarding the creative processes of the garden as a *servant*.

> Now the *serpent* was more subtle than any beast of the field which the Lord God had made. And he said unto the woman, Yea, hath God said, Ye shall not eat of every tree in the garden? And the woman said unto the serpent, We may eat of the fruit of the trees of the garden: But of the fruit of the tree which is in the midst of the garden, God hath said, Ye shall not eat of it, neither shall ye touch it, lest ye die. And the serpent said unto the woman, Ye shall not surely die: For God doth know that in the day ye eat thereof, then your eyes shall be opened, and ye shall be as gods knowing good and evil.
>
> Genesis 3: 1-5

THE SERPENT IS THE SENSE OF SELF, THE SENSE

OF INDIVIDUAL IDENTITY THAT INHABITED THE MIND/BRAINS OF THE FIRST HUMANS.

There was nothing inherently wrong with this serpent. It was supposed to be there in the branches of the tree. It symbolizes the graceful nature of healthy human identity. If you have ever watched a snake crawling across the ground or climbing up a tree, you have noticed that it flows; it undulates, it weaves back and forth. The serpent protrays the fluid sense of self that inhabited the first humans, a sense of self that gracefully rode the precise balance point between spirit and matter that met in each conscious human mind. Such an identity honors both mother and father. It embodies an easy balance of material essences becoming spiritualized, and spiritual essences in a process of incarnation. It embodies the same kind of easy balance that a child who knows how to ride a two-wheeled bicycle experiences; the balancing is unconscious. It is extremely awkward when it becomes conscious.

By eating of the fruit of the tree of the knowledge of good and evil, the first humans became suddenly conscious of the immensity of all the dimensions of spirit and matter that were being balanced through their individual senses of identity. They were overwhelmed. Suddenly they found themselves aware of all the infinite detail that went into the maintenance of a proper balance. They had made an autonomic process conscious.

Remember learning to ride a two wheeled bicycle? You know the intense concentration that went into your first efforts. So many things to think of simultaneously; adjusting for the pull of gravity this way, adjusting for the pull of gravity that way, compensating for a dip in the road or a pebble, trying to regulate your speed and steer at the same time—and all the while plagued by a fear of falling. It was incredibly awkward. But one day something clicked. You got into a flow with it, you caught the spirit of the thing and it soon became second nature; you no longer had to worry about a thousand and one details. It had become autonomic.

The story of the Fall is a tale of this process in reverse. The long record of human history with its pain, conflict, misery and alienation is not simply the story of a race new to the physical plane, engaged in a process of natural learning. Humanity's true learning was to have been in another realm altogther. No, the bitter-sweet tragedy of human history did not have to occur. If we would break the spell of its ignorance and step outside the range of its illusions, it might pay us to take a closer look at this serpent nestled in the branches of the tree.

"MORE SUBTLE THAN
ANY BEAST OF THE FIELD"

The challenge before the first humans was to honor both spirit and matter, while making sure that all motivation came from spirit. If motivation came from matter at this point, it would lead back into matter; for matter's understanding of herself back in those early days was still associated with specific structure. The matter suspended in the energy fields of each human creature was still thinking of itself as disassociated from the entirety of the earth, as something separate and distinct. This was as it should have been. It was not, however, to have been a source of motivation. If identities that thought of themselves as isolated from everything around them were to play roles in decision-making, the resulting decisions would lack overall coordination. Conflict would be inevitable.

Human subjectivity was eventually to have had motivational input, but only after a training period during which a fuller blending of spirit nature and earth nature would take place. Never should an aspect of identity that perceived itself as separate from God dictate behavior. When the first humans began using the mind/brains in the midst of their physical bodies to determine good and evil, they were usurping the prerogatives of God and cutting themselves off from a source of common direction. When they began to evaluate the relative goods and evils of their various behavioral options from a center of consciousness that imagined itself as separate from everything around it, they were assuming authority they were in no way ready for.

The truth was, these early humans did not know what was good for them and what was not. A parent is aware of the necessity of keeping a two-year-old out of the turpentine or away from the hot stove. Various external controls are utilized to keep the child from getting hurt through experiences that the child, in its ignorance, might perceive as "good." In the case of the first humans, the control was to have been internal; God instructed them not to use their subjective minds to *determine basic spiritual motivation.* There was nothing wrong with the first humans using their subjective minds for day-to-day decisions. But basic spiritual motivation was something different.

Basic spiritual motivation pertains to long-term directions and priorities. It has to do with determining objectives and underlying purposes. It relates to one's talents, inclinations and creative tendencies. It has to do with the basic purpose of one's life.

TO OVERRIDE ONE'S FUNDAMENTAL LIFE PUR-POSE THROUGH THE SUPERIMPOSITION OF SOME COURSE OF ACTION DETERMINED BY A SUBJEC-TIVE THOUGHT PROCESS IS TO EAT OF THE FOR-BIDDEN FRUIT.

Each individual has a specific purpose for being on this earth. This is as true today as it was in the garden. This purpose may contain numerous sub-purposes, but there is only one fundamental purpose for each human being. Like the branches of a tree, these individual purposes all join at the trunk of the Creator's larger purpose on earth.

God's purpose shines down upon the earth much like the sun. In the realm of heaven, where all form exists in essence, God's purpose is differentiated like light through a series of prisms; it becomes an individual purpose for each human being.

THE ANIMATING CURRENT OR LIFE ENERGY AVAILABLE TO EACH OF US SPRINGS DIRECTLY FROM OUR INDIVIDUAL PURPOSE.

I am sure that you have had the experience sometime or

another of driving down the road late one foggy evening when your vehicle's headlights cast a distinct beam into the blackness ahead. The area illuminated by your headlights in this analogy could be seen as the range of your life's purpose, the range where energy is available to you. To demonstrate this, park your imaginary car and step back and forth in and out of the light beam projected by the car's headlights. Like a solar cell, you will notice your energy increase and decrease in direct proportion to how much of you is receiving the light.

In the fallen state most people are only partially aligned with their life's purpose. They receive life energy only to the degree of their alignment. Overriding their life purposes, they remove themselves from the range of function where their energy is available; their vitality cannot help but diminish. Ultimately, death is the penalty for persisting in such folly. "For in the day that thou eatest thereof, thou shalt surely die."

When the first man and the first woman ate of the fruit of the tree of the knowledge of good and evil, they took it upon themselves to expend greatly the range of their subjective input. They began making major motivational decisions based on fragmentary data.

Their individual range of perception and comprehension could not possibly be aware of all the factors affected by these decisions. Consequently, their individual purposes became distorted and were no longer in harmony with the other life-forms of the garden. Conflict was initiated.

> And when the woman saw that the tree was good for food, and that it was pleasant to the eyes, and a tree to be desired to make one wise, she took of the fruit thereof, and did eat, and gave also unto her husband with her; and he did eat. And the eyes of them both were opened . . .
>
> Genesis 3: 6-7

The graceful fluid sense of identity that was to ride the fluctuating balance between spirit and matter in individual consciousness, fell, like a child off a bicycle, toward the gravity of earth. For the first time, gravity began to affect consciousness; things began to look grave. The easy and natural provision of the earth began to be called into question by fallen spirits whose eyes were indeed open. They became aware of what they suddenly perceived as "the tenuous nature of their life support systems." No longer trusting in God and in the ability of the earth to provide, they became afraid.

OVERWHELMED BY A PHYSICAL PLANE

Suppose a young air force cadet is taken up into one of our modern jet fighters for training. He finds himself seated beside his trainer, an experienced pilot, facing an extremely complex control panel. He has had a bit of textbook training, but this is his first time off the ground. He may be looking forward to the day when he can take full control of the plane himself, but we assume he knows how vital it is that he allow his trainer to actually operate the controls for a period of time while he listens and watches. If suddenly he were to assume full control of the plane and at the same time to lose all contact with his trainer, he would likely find himself overwhelmed.

The Creator maintained contact with the first humans in the garden through their love and through their trust. When they ate of the forbidden fruit and their eyes were open, suddenly they became aware of the immensity of their responsibility and their own lack of preparedness. The full implications of their position in the creative scheme of things were to gradually become revealed to them in the course of their training. When the full implications came upon them all at once with the simultaneous realization that they had ignored one of God's primary instructions, they became afraid, afraid of their awesome responsibility and afraid of God's anger. Their connection with God had been through their love of God and now they assumed they had reason to fear him.

THEIR FEAR CHURNED UP STATIC ON THE FREQUENCIES WHERE GOD'S VOICE WAS AUDIBLE. THEY SUDDENLY LOST CONTACT.

The serpent in the tree in the midst of the garden was to have undergone a period of training as a *servant*. Only when it had done what it had been commanded to do for a period, would it rightly have graduated into friendship and have been offered the kind of participatory role that it prematurely usurped. Centuries later Jesus was to speak the words to a few close disciples that could have been spoken sooner under much brighter circumstances.

> Ye are my friends if ye do whatsoever I command you. Henceforth I call you not servants; for the servant knoweth not what his lord doeth; but I have called you friends; for all things that I have heard of my Father I have made known unto you.
>
> John 15: 14-15

Once certain basics were conveyed, once the larger purposes of the Creator were made known to the humans in the garden, once they understood what their Creator was about, then they would have graduated into friendship with God. It would have been appropriate then to use their sensory apparatus for certain kinds of decision-making. They would have known then what was fitting, what was in harmony with the overall purposes of creation.

WHEN THEIR EYES WERE OPEN "AND THEY KNEW" PREMATURELY, THEY BECAME OVERWHELMED BY THE INPUT OF THEIR FIVE PHYSICAL SENSES.

They did indeed, as the serpent said, become as gods knowing good and evil, but they were not grounded yet, they were not ready for it. They gave far too much weight to what their physical senses were telling them. Through their fear, shame and guilt, they set up semi-permanent emotional turbulence in their surrounding atmosphere which cut them off from their spiritual senses.

They became so enamored of their physical clothing, they forgot their living spirits within.

Their spiritual bodies became imperceptible and "they knew that they were naked." They were painfully aware of their unpreparedness. "They sewed fig leaves together, and made themselves aprons." They tried to hide their nakedness. When God came walking in the garden looking for them, they hid behind the trees of the garden. They used their minds to justify, to rationalize. They hid behind aprons of concept and belief. They used their physical senses as a barrier between themselves and God.

PHYSICAL SENSITIVITIES SOON BECAME THE ONLY FREQUENCY TO WHICH HUMAN BEINGS WERE ATTUNED.

Like a radio stuck on the weather frequency, unable to turn to any other, human beings locked out perception of whole dimensions of spiritual input and began making decisions based on fragmented data. All the finer frequencies were ignored or forgotten in their growing infatuation with form.

Like a deep sea diver who has become so intent on examining the undersea coral that he forgets his diving suit is just a temporary housing for his body with a limited supply of air, human beings forgot their source in the air of eternal spirit. They forgot to come up into spirit to recharge their souls. The body and its attendant priorities no longer occupied a balanced place in their motivation. It began to dominate and control.

The individual, thinking of him or herself as a separate isolated entity, perceiving through sensory apparatus heavily dominated by physical senses, can no longer be guided through direct communion with God. He or she now has to be shepherded from experience to experience, slowly and patiently guided down the long and winding road which has become recorded human history. Fortunately, during their long and harrowing journey, humankind was not forgotten.

III

THE INTERIM

THE GOOD SHEPHERD
AND AN INTIMATE CONVERSATION

It was the darkest hour of the human drama. Ignorance covered the face of the land. Every man did what was right in his own eyes. Conflict abounded. Cain, one of Adam and Eve's own children, did the unthinkable: he destroyed his brother Abel's physical body.

IMMEDIATELY AFTER THE MURDER, CAIN BUILT THE FIRST CITY.

The city proved an ideal location for fearful human creatures to store the grains thay had wrestled from the grasp of a hostile biosphere. But in the cities the people did not know how to treat one another civilly. Like iron filings drawn into a magnetic field, customs and traditions began to structure themselves along the underlying currents of human fear. Artificial codes of so-called "ethics" were arbitrarily enforced to minimize violence, at least during commercial transactions. From the cities, civilizations* began to spill over into the surrounding countryside. Outside the context of civilization, the few remaining hunting and gathering peoples embodied the very best—for indirect contact with God was sometimes possible—and they embodied the very worst, at times sinking to levels of open depravity on a scale not usually possible in the cities.

Within the civilized world, new languages grew up, languages based on commerce, trade, conquest and victory.

Civilization: From the Latin root word "civitas" which means city.

Human beings were conditioned to consider only those things which neatly fit into the local language as being real, including definitions of themselves. The roles and relationships that developed during this dark period were based on assumptions. The underlying assumption was that a hostile environment would not provide enough to meet the needs of everyone, so obviously there must be winners—and losers.

But still some human hearts longed. Some kept a vague memory of another, earlier time, before cities. A few kept written records. God did not leave these comfortless. He had not forgotten them; He had devised an ingenious protection plan for those who still remembered and still loved. Most of the civilized humans were too preoccupied with the petty details of their material survival to sense or intuit what this divine protection plan might be.

But not everyone. A few still looked to heaven.

David was sitting on the side of a grassy hill. Far below him was a small village nestled in the fertile hills of the Jordan River Valley. His responsibilities left him with time to think. Every so often he would get up and guide a few of his family's wandering sheep back into the fold. It was David's habit (as it was a general custom of shepherds in those days) always to lead the sheep, never to drive them. So two or three times a day, he would lead his sheep to other sections of the hillside. Whenever his active periods were over, he would resume a sitting position on the hill above the sheep. This particular afternoon was warm and sunny. A gentle breeze blew a few cumulus clouds across the sky. David was deep in thought.

The evening before he had gathered with a few believers in one of the houses. Someone had read. He had heard the words many times before, but last night something had struck a deep chord in him. The passage was running through his mind again. "And they heard the voice of the Lord God walking in the garden in the cool of the day: and Adam and his wife hid themselves . . . amongst the trees in the garden." David imagined the Lord God walking in the garden in the cool of the day. He would not have hidden himself. No, he would have run out to greet the Lord like a lover and a friend. Yes, even if he had sinned, so what? David still trusted God. He would rush out to Him; he would make it up then and there.

Even now David felt the Lord's spirit with him, watching over him and his activities, just as he was watching over his sheep. "The Lord is my shepherd," David thought, "though I can't hear His voice or see His form or reach out to touch Him as I so long to do. Still, He watches over me. I shall not want." He was glad he had brought writing implements. He carefully opened a tiny vial containing the dark juice of the berries he had mashed the previous evening. He dipped his quill and began to write:

> The Lord is my shepherd; I shall not want. He maketh me to lie down in green pastures: he leadeth me beside the still waters. He restoreth my soul: he leadeth me in the paths of righteousness for his name's sake.
>
> Yea, though I walk through the valley of the shadow of death, I will fear no evil: for thou art with me; thy rod and thy staff they comfort me.
>
> Thou preparest a table before me in the presence of mine enemies: thou anointest my head with oil; my cup runneth over.
>
> Surely goodness and mercy shall follow me all the days of my life: and I will dwell in the house of the Lord for ever.

Twenty-third Psalm

My wife, Sherry, was reading the words. We were sitting on a gently sloping grassy hill. Unlike David's pasture, it was surrounded by miles of forest. It was a warm Sunday afternoon. How nice it was to live in the woods, so far from the distractions of the busy commercial world! The trees at the foot of the hill were as still as the air around us. Our nearest neighbor was a mile away, the nearest highway, far to the south. The only sound was Sherry's voice, punctuated occasionally by a distant woodpecker or the lazy buzzing of a fly.

When she had finished reading, neither of us said anything.

It was good just to be there together in the rich silence. Finally, as if with sudden inspiration, Sherry spoke, "You know, it seems that there are two ways of being in God's presence. I seem to drift back and forth between them. Sometimes I experience myself as a part of God. I feel Christ living in my heart. I really know who I am. I know I'm a connected branch of the vine, an aspect of the Creator, dressed up in this particular body, mind and heart. I'm in touch with my deeper purpose and I know exactly what I'm supposed to be doing. But other times, it's like I'm in a fog. I feel confused. Often tired. I don't see things clearly. I know that God is still inside of me, of course, but I don't experience it consciously anymore. I trust that a time will come when I'll be able to feel him within me again, but during these foggy times, God seems far away. It can be terribly lonely."

I said that I felt like that too from time to time. "I think that's just the way it's going to be throughout this transition period. There seems to be a natural ebb and flow to our awakening. It gives us time to incorporate God's vision into our everyday lives."

"Oh I know periods of assimilation are necessary," Sherry continued. "It's like inbreathing and outbreathing. What I was getting at was the value of the Shepherd's Psalm during the foggy times. It is such a powerful statement of truth. It's like an insurance policy, guaranteeing that everything is just as it should be, assuring us that everything is working out to ultimate perfection."

"A sort of divine protection plan?"

"Exactly. As long as an individual does his or her best *everything else is taken care of! God assures us that we will be provided with everything we require.* There is never any cause to worry about anything, every *real* need is taken care of."

"What do you mean though by doing your best? That sounds kind of ambiguous."

"As long as you are honest with yourself, as long as your motivation springs from your own highest vision, God takes care of everything else—right down to the eggs in the refrigerator. 'The Lord is my shepherd; I shall not want.' The

23rd Psalm describes the great safety net that lies beneath all those who make the decision to walk with God and never again be motivated by fear. To whatever degree people don't understand all this kind of stuff we're talking about, to whatever degree we ourselves forget it from time to time, our hearts need not be troubled nor afraid; for God knows of our needs. As long as we're doing our best, He's there to take up the slack. He covers for us until we're able to be conscious all the time. One only needs to trust in God. The worst that can happen is 'The Lord is my shepherd.' He guides and protects me. 'I shall not want.' I won't go without anything that I truly require. 'He maketh me to lie down in green pastures.' You know, when I'm not real clear. Say I can't make head nor tail of my motivation. Well, it's OK. It's all part of the awakening process. I relax, trust in God, and as long as I do my best, no matter how short of perfection that may turn out to be, I'm assured that God will 'maketh me to lie down in green pastures. He leadeth me beside still waters.' My heart remains untroubled. The still waters reflect the light of God. It is near the still waters that the Spirit of truth finds people. When the heart is untroubled, the emotional realm becomes like a sea of glass clear as crystal; its stillness is sensitive to God's spirit."

"It sure is vital to continue trusting in God."

"It's the most important thing! No matter what happens, as long as one trusts, everything works out just fine, because the connection with God is maintained. Even if you're not always consciously aware of it, it's maintained in the heart. Then, 'He restoreth my soul: he leadeth me in the paths of righteousness for his name's sake.' When the waters of awareness are untroubled by worry and concern, the soul is restored, healed, made whole. One is led down the paths of righteousness, instructed in the right use of mind and emotions.

" 'Yea though I walk through the valley of the shadow of death, I will fear no evil: for thou art with me; thy rod and thy staff they comfort me.'

"No matter what happens, no matter how bleak mental

descriptions of my situation may cause things to appear, I won't lose faith or let my heart be troubled. Though I incarnate physically and suddenly find myself immersed in a realm where forms and identities come and go and there seems to be a kind of death, a termination of form, I will fear no evil. Why should I? 'Thy rod and thy staff they comfort me.' I know that I have a deeper identity in God. Forms continuously come and go. There really isn't any continuity of specific form in either earth or sun. Biological life rises and falls. Spirit is fluid. 'Though I walk through the valley of the shadow of death,' though I see the possibility before me, I will fear no ... what? rebirth? transmutation? If it occurs, it occurs, I will fear no evil. I know that so long as I trust in God and align my purposes with His, my days in this form will be just what they ought to be. I rest, comfortable in the assurance of God's presence within me and around me, imbuing everything I perceive, making this incarnate perspective possible."

Sherry and I looked at each other and both of us started to laugh. Our conversation was taking an interesting turn. We decided to continue on through the rest of the 23rd Psalm in the same spirit and see what God might show us. Sherry continued to have most of the inspiration.

" 'He preparest a table before me,' " she continued, " 'in the presence of mine enemies: He anointest my head with oil; my cup runneth over.' Enemies in this case might be seen as false descriptions of my situation, trying to provoke fear-motivated behavior. But on the table right in the midst of these endless reasons why I should be afraid is a feast—not just everything I need, but a veritable feast. 'My cup runneth over!' For those who trust in God, no matter how hostile their local description-of-reality deities may appear, God prepares a feast. He doesn't necessarily change the descriptions or make them go away. Right in the midst of them, right in the midst of what might well appear to be chaos and turmoil, He 'anointest my head with oil.' He blesses the trusting with the oil of His love. His peace permeates the atmosphere. Everything required is provided."

I hated to interrupt for such a mundane analogy, but I had

seen a movie once (I can not remember now if it was Peter Sellers or Bob Hope) I wanted to tell Sherry about. It took place shortly after the occupation of Berlin at the close of World War II. Two soldiers were sitting in the middle of a totally bombed-out city, in an old decrepit building with just one wall left half-standing. Somehow they had come across a couple of extra cases of K rations and a few bottles of French wine. They were sitting there a bit bombed out themselves (the more I think about this the more I am sure it was one of those Bob Hope/Bing Crosby movies). A couple of the local frauleins had joined them, and they were having the time of their lives. Every so often a nearby explosion would dislodge a few more bricks from the wall behind them, but they were totally unperturbed, enjoying themselves immensely, eating and drinking as if there were not a war going on.

Sherry smiled as I related this, but she did not have quite my enthusiasm for the analogy. I let her continue.

" 'Thou anointest my head with oil.' All the tangled, worried, confused survival concerns of the rational mind are anointed with the oil of divine love. 'My cup runneth over.' Everything I need is provided, and then even more is given. 'Surely goodness and mercy shall follow me all the days of my life.' Everywhere I go, goodness and mercy are following in my wake, fanning out into the environment around me. Because of my trust in God and for no other reason, the design of the universe is being manifest through me."

Sherry looked up. "Now, personally, I wouldn't describe my experience on earth as a walk through the valley of the shadow of death, but there have been scary times and I'm sure there are scary times for each of us. During these scary times, when the truth might not seem very accessible, the simple invitation nevertheless remains: put your trust in God. It's even printed on the back of our money! Wherever trust in God prevails in spite of all seeming adversity, prosperity is close behind. 'Surely goodness and mercy shall follow me all the days of my life and I will dwell in the house of the Lord for ever.' "

She closed the Bible. Neither of us spoke. It would have been superfluous. We had both been deeply touched by

David's words. Perhaps human language had some redeeming features; it had certainly called a magic to us from across the centuries.

After a brief moment of silence, Sherry rose to her feet and walked off toward the barn to do the evening milking. I watched her walk through the garden in the middle of our clearing. The clearing itself was surrounded by miles of forest.

"It seems balanced this way." I thought, "Surely some agriculture is part of tending and keeping the Garden. Perhaps it would not have developed in such a methodical and unhealthy way, though, if it had not been for cities . . . . "

But I did not pursue the thought. I was feeling too much emotion.

IMAGES OF THE FALLEN WORLD

In looking around this beautiful planet that we are privileged to call home, we see many things that are not as we inherently sense they should be. We see people going without adequate food, clothing and shelter. We see short-term industrial priorities wreaking havoc with delicate ecologies. We see the threat of nuclear war lingering ever more noticeably on the horizon. We are beset by such a range of crises that some analysts have simply lumped them all together to refer to our present global condition as a "megacrisis." Yet we are not without recourse.

IF THERE IS A MEGACRISIS, THERE IS ALSO A MEGAOPPORTUNITY.

Every crisis is a call to re-evaluate and adjust behavior. The Chinese sum it up in the single word, "wei-chi." The first part of the word, "wei," means danger, beware. The second part of the word, "chi," means great opportunity. The last century has seen many people respond to the opportunity by joining various issue-related groups and organizations. These efforts are laudable; they may alleviate symptoms for a time; but for the most part, they are far from adequate. The causes of discontent remain. The problems keep on growing. As Thoreau once commented, "There are a thousand striking at the branches of evil for every one who is striking at the root."

Is it not evident that human behavior itself lies at the root of the megacrisis? It is people who have created these crises, people who have created situations of conflict, misunderstanding, greed, overconsumption, poverty, violence, and the rest.

We are witnessing the manifold results of a fundamental human malfunction. Our megaopportunity, it would seem, is to examine the cause of this basic malfunction and see what might be done about it.

There is evidence that the roots of conflict and suffering lie in our habitual and rarely challenged processes of decision-making. We know that prior to any outer action is a thought process. Could it be that there is something inherently wrong with the way that we have been trained to use our minds? Is there a way in which we can approach our processes of thought differently?

All logical thought is based upon initial assumptions. If these assumptions are inaccurate, it follows that the end results of thought based upon them might magnify the inaccuracies many times. A telescope aimed at the distant stars has only to move a few millimeters at its base to move the point of its focus many light years across the heavens. In much the same way, the destructive end results of thought processes based on erroneous premises can magnify their initial errors many thousands of times. Perhaps you recall the dream that Daniel interpreted for King Nebuchadnezzar.

> Thou, O king, sawest and beheld a great image.
> This image whose brightness was excellent,
> **stood before thee; and the form thereof was**
> **terrible. This image's head was of fine gold, his**
> **breast and his arms of silver, his belly and his**
> thighs of brass. His legs were of iron, his feet,
> part of iron and part of clay. Thou sawest that
> a stone was cut out without hands which smote
> the image upon his feet that were of iron and
> clay and brake them to pieces.

> Daniel 2: 31-34

This image is often seen as a metaphor for the civilized world, a showy head of fine gold resting on unsteady feet of clay. Personally, I regard the image in Nebuchadnezzar's dream as a graphic symbol of typical human thought processes. Their conclusions and overall brightness often appear excellent (a head of fine gold). Their supporting logic (breast and arms of silver) are often flawless, superbly built upon good solid data (belly and thighs of brass). But when we get down to some of the assumptions behind all this logic, we find nothing more than brittle iron legs supported by feet (symbolizing understanding) part of iron and part of clay.

The entire edifice of contemporary logic is resting on an unstable premise. Yet this premise had endured unquestioned at the root of individual and societal behavior for thousands of years. Individuals and their civilizations have unsuccessfully attempted to construct lasting achievement upon it. Only shallow and superficial accomplishment has resulted, however, purchased at exorbitant cost to themselves and to the earth. Eventually "the stone cut out without hands" smites all such precarious edifices on their feet of clay. The erroneous premise upon which we base virtually our every thought is simply a mistaken way of thinking of ourselves.

AS LONG AS WE CONCEIVE OF OURSELVES AS SEPARATE, ISOLATED INDIVIDUALS, OUR THOUGHT PROCESSES WILL NEVER BE TRULY LOGICAL BECAUSE THEY WILL CONTINUE TO SPRING FROM AN ILLOGICAL PREMISE.

Until we *experience* ourselves as integrated members of a single, interwoven, biological and spiritual family, everything we think, say and do, no matter how well motivated, will be subject to fundamental distortion. Before we are capable of creative thought, we must *experience ourselves* in the context of the whole.

This was impressed upon me recently as I walked along the edge of a nearby creek after a refreshing spring shower. Watching the curious formations that appeared in the water as it flowed past, I was struck by one particular eddy whirling around in an oval facial pattern. I wondered how it might be defined. I mean—what was it *really*? The specific molecules of water that made it visible were only held in its current for a moment or two before they were whisked downstream. Technically speaking, it had to be more than simply water. I began to realize that what I was seeing could not possibly be defined in isolation; it could not be understood apart from the whole of the creek and the landscape through which the creek was moving.

It was easy to see parallels. I thought of the matter flowing in and out of my own body. I knew I was not the cells that were continuously being created and destroyed within me. Why, most of my cells had been replaced hundreds of times since I had been a child. Even the most stubborn part of my anatomy, my collagen, had come and gone a half dozen times. "I," whatever I was, was clearly distinct from the matter passing through me.

This is obvious when we speak of our physical bodies, but for most of us it has been less obvious in regard to the contents of our minds. A child's identity will change dramatically, healthily, from one year to the next. But how often does an adult's sense of self change? Should not images and perception continuously be flowing in and out of a healthy mind just as matter is continuously flowing in and out of a healthy body?

Identifying with the contents of consciousness is as foolish as a whirlpool defining itself as the water passing through. Human beings cannot separate themselves from the flowing River of Life any more than a scientist could surgically remove a whirlpool from a river in order to examine it more closely. Like the leaves of a tree or the blossoms of a vine, each of us is an integral part of a larger whole. It is impossible to separate an individual human being from the interwoven fabric of the whole of terrestrial life.

One cannot, *in fact*, separate oneself from earth or spirit. However, *the illusion* of separate identity can be maintained. Human beings *can imagine* that they are separate from the surrounding flow of time and space. On rare occasions there may be a place for this, but it is meant to be a conscious option, not an involuntary historical condition.

True identity is fluid; it gracefully meets the contours of each changing moment with the particular qualities of character that it brings to focus. It does not cling to passing images and perceptions; it lets them flow through and turns to greet the fresh content that is ever-moving into the range of its awareness, never forgetting that its immediate individuality is rooted in an expression of wholeness.

THE CONSISTENCY OF TRUE IDENTITY LIES IN THE *ORGANIZATION* OF CONSCIOUSNESS, NOT IN THE *CONTENTS* OF CONSCIOUSNESS.

When an individual becomes so fixated upon an image of him or herself that he or she is unable to let go of it when that image needs to pass on, that individual begins to die. Life-giving energy is mischanneled into an arbitrary structure that must then continuously struggle against the flow of time. The rigid self image becomes a sort of warped vibrational field that is capable of drawing the very cells of the body into its incongruities.

At the root of fallen human assumptions is the premise that we are *essentially* separate from our mother's earth and our father's spirit. Taking on separate identities can be as natural as wearing clothes, but such identities are never to motivate behavior. The results of such subjective-motivation are as chaotic as a suit of clothes walking away with the unconscious owner inside or an actor continuing to dramatize a role long after the production had ended. As long as thinking springs from a sense of self that is unaware of its connection with the whole, the resulting behavior will be out of season, out of place.

We can break the Second Commandment as it was given to Moses on Mount Sinai by making images and likenesses of ourselves and worshipping them through the investment of our very sense of self, but we will not thrive in such a condition. We will, in effect, be writing our own tickets to extinction. It is precisely such false identification—unconsciously sustained—that lies at the root of conflict, sorrow, and every human evil.

So we continue our journey, looking upon all that we have considered in these pages as transitional structures of thought flowing in and out of our attention, much as specific molecules of water might flow in and out of a whirlpool along the edge of our favorite river. Gradually the rhythm of our thought is beginning to pulsate with the tempo of God's own understanding. Like gears meshing when a clutch is released, a time will come when the conceptual content of our consciousness will find itself reorganized along the lines of our Maker's comprehension.

IV

A T T U N E M E N T

OUR NATIVE FREQUENCIES

There is something hauntingly beautiful about the evening of the day, the lengthening shadows, the coolness rising up from the valleys, the sun descending in splendor beneath the horizon, the appearance of the first star, the first twilight song of a whippoorwill, the distant hoot of an owl. It is not difficult to cast our minds back in imagination to a time when the Creator of all this wonder might have walked in the garden in the cool of the day, a time prior to the fall of human consciousness when creative intelligence still flowed gracefully through an integrated human family, a time when clarity, precision and joy wrote the order of the ages.

It is a privilege to live in an age when we can once more become conscious, understanding because we love, loving because it is our nature to do so. To the extent that we are unafraid to allow the creative passion of a holy and universal spirit to activate our perceptions, we begin to see our Lord and Maker behind every pair of eyes we look into, in every situation, every circumstance, every moment. To the extent that we begin to re-experience ourselves as aspects of One Living Spirit, we begin to recognize that spirit in all we perceive. The interpretations of the past no longer hold us quite so tightly in their illusions.

We begin to see beyond the surface of our events. Increasingly, we are aware of *cause*. We still have subjective preferences, but we observe them, no longer addicted to their demands. As we continue in the healing process, our subjective desires begin to fall away like blinders that have obscured our vision. The doors of our perception are opened to God. His vision re-creates our world.

We see that the law works, that ignorance begets ignorance, that the sowing of reactive seeds causes the reaping of experiences to help us learn and change. Eventually we come to realize that behind all appearances, the universe is unfolding as it should. An inexorable love is healing and cleansing, drawing all things slowly to perfection—not the static perfection of the frozen and immobile, but the fluid perfection of a universe growing like a summer garden or a healthy child. Sensing the perfection that remains even in our fallen world, behind and within, we begin to live in a new heaven. We find ourselves increasingly drawn to situations where love is active. We apprehend a new earth.

We see the garden that was once obscured from human vision. We become re-connected with the spirit behind our own life, the spirit *of* Life that we are. Perhaps at last, we begin to perceive the outworking of our particular historical era for what it is. We are living in a time anticipated by the folk traditions of the earth's every people, a time when the convergence of many factors is beginning to make possible the healing of our planet and her nations.

To help us participate more effectively in the opportunities and challenges that present themselves to us at the sunset of one epoch and the dawn of a greater, we might take a look at a process called *attunement.*

One of the first images that comes to mind when hearing the word "attunement" is the image of someone tuning a musical instrument. This is a useful image. When a piano is out of tune, it does not matter how accomplished the pianist is who attempts to play it; if the music sounds discordant and clashing, we do not blame the pianist. Yet when people blame God for the problems of the earth, their accusations are just as irrational. The problems that appear on earth are not due to the intelligence of the Life that moves through human bodies, minds and hearts. The problems are due to the fact that these human systems are themselves not properly tuned. There are specific vibrational frequencies within the range of humankind's designated arena of function upon which each individual is designed to function. Attunement is the process of re-sensitizing our bodies, minds and hearts to these, our native frequencies.

A WORLD OF TANGIBLE SOUND

Physics classes will often conduct experiments with pure tones, observing their effects on various media: sand, oil, water, etc. Participating in these on occasion, I have seen sand arrange itself in precise geometric formation when the bow of a violin was drawn across the tin plate on which it was resting. I have seen certain tones cause oil floating on the surface of water to coagulate into cell-like configurations that seemed to grow and divide like amoeba as the tone's pitch was slowly raised, I have seen tiny grains of salt stand one upon the other and dance like human figures as they experienced a vibrating surface beneath them.

Physicists, attempting to determine the precise nature of this physical stuff that we call matter have probed deeper and deeper into the realms of atomic and subatomic behavior only to find that there is nothing there, at least no "thing" in the sense in which we normally think of matter. They describe the tiniest subatomic particles as "interference patterns of various sound frequencies." They call them "nodes of resonance."

The nucleus of each atom is made up of these "nodes of resonance." Each atom is itself vibrating at a phenomenal rate of up to ten to the fourteenth power times per second, emitting a single note about twenty octaves *above* the range of our hearing. Seismographs pick up minor, but consistent tremors of the earth, with vibration periods every 53.1 and 54.7 minutes. These mini-earthquakes produce a tone about twenty octaves *below* the range of our hearing. Existing midway between the subatomic sopranos and the planetary basses, human beings inhabit a world of tangible sound.

Perhaps Pythagoras was on to something 2,500 years ago when he suggested that matter was actually "frozen music."

Even the electrochemical activity of the brain is directed and organized by subtle wave vibrations. Our five physical senses are each rooted in vibration. Perception of light too is a vibratory event. When you glance for a single second at the yellow leaves of an autumnal elm, the dye molecules in the retina of your eye vibrate 500 trillion times—more waves in that single second than all the ocean waves that have beat upon the earth's shores since the first morning of creation.

Vibration is found at the root of every phenomenon; but in a fallen world, not all sound affects us equally. There are discharged sounds that deplete human energy as well as charged sounds that bring us strength and vitality. The power of these charged sounds is illustrated by Benedictine monks who have found that they can go for years on no more than three hours sleep per night *provided they chant six to eight hours each day.* When the length of their chanting is shortened, their need for sleep increases proportionately.

The same mechanism that allows us to hear a portion of the sound spectrum provides us with our sense of balance. It is the very same ear with which we listen to our world that provides us with our alignment to the earth's gravity.

At the fluid point of balance between time and eternity, our mind/brains face the opportunity of replicating all creation in specified dimensional terms. When resonance occurs, we sense the creative first sound with every breath and feel a timeless purpose with every beat of the heart.

Within us, around us, the music of the spheres unfolds in rhythms celestial and melodies terrestrial. More than just the hills are alive with music. Matter and light themselves are secondary aspects of sound. The phenomenal structure inherent in every tone emerges as the first expression of reality formation.

> In the beginning was the word, and the word
> was with God and the Word was God.

> John 1: 1

In the beginning was the creative sound, the primal tone, that contained within it every sound, symphony, harmony and melody, every pattern and structure ever to be. The Word that *was* with God has not ceased to be; this very moment, it holds suspended within its vibratory magnificence, every atom, molecule, cell and organism. It sings the very earth into being. The sun, moon and planets share in a symphony of the heavens that includes every comet, asteroid and star-system in our galaxy—and in a billion others. In this beginning *is* the Word. The Word *is* with God. And the Word *is* God. The Word brings each of us into dimensional expression.

RESONANCE:
A GENERATION'S OPPORTUNITY

The Word that is spoken by God resounds in our mutual hearing simultaneously. This eternal, creative moment opens the arms of her potential inviting harmony and grace. In a linear sense, as we approach the end of this century, each moment becomes *more welcoming*. As each additional human being enters a state of healthy attunement, it becomes easier for others to enter into harmony with them. Though the opportunity to experience a fundamental spiritual healing has always been present, it has never been so easy. It is becoming easier day by day.

It has been said that every Christian generation has had among its numbers those who supposed they were to see the Second Coming, that the Christians of the late twentieth century are merely echoing the hope that springs fresh in every age. Yet even without taking into account the prophecies which point to modern times, there is a profound reason why you and I are living in the generation that shall see the restored dominion of God's creative purposes upon the earth. This reason can be summed up in four words: *the power of attunement.*

Putting all other factors aside for a moment, the laws of probability suggest that as the earth's population continues to increase, each given moment will find more people than ever before in a state of harmonious function. Every human being who begins to function in a healthy way enters "the Holy Place of the Most High," a state of attunement with the full spectrum of vibrational frequencies that dance throughout the universal order. Each individual who restores trust in God sounds a note in harmonic resonance with the entire cosmos. This magnifies the vibrations of the Holy Place.

Presently, each human being on earth is sounding a note or tone of sorts, but for the most part these notes are not in any kind of harmony. Just as no two snowflakes are alike, no two discordant notes are ever similar enough to build upon one another's harmonics. Consequently, their destructive effects on the surrounding environment are arithmetically cumulative, but far from exponential. If it were possible for dissonance to become amplified through resonance, the earth would have long since perished.

Many a bridge collapsed beneath the coordinated step of marching soldiers before the awesome power of resonance was recognized. Physicists call this curious amplification of harmonics "rhythmic entrainment." Perhaps the best example of it was discovered by the proprietors of 19th century clock shops who repeatedly observed that all their clocks with pendulums of the same length would sooner or later end up with their pendulums swinging in harmony. Experiments showed that no matter how randomly the pendulums were set in motion, sooner or later, they would all begin swinging together. Moreover, it was found that the length of time that it took for all the pendulums to begin swinging in harmony (after they were set in motion randomly) *decreased exponentially* in direct proportion to the number of clocks that had begun to move together. In other words, it would take a while for the first two clocks out of a roomful of forty-five clocks to begin to swing together once the pendulums of all forty-five clocks had been randomly set in motion. It would not take quite so long for the third clock to join the first two. The fourth would come in with much less hesitation and so on, until by the time there were (say) a dozen clocks with pendulums swinging side by side, it would seem that the rest would join them almost instantaneously. The number that it takes to cause this almost instantaneous shift of the whole is called "a resonant minority."

No one who has lived during the two millennia since the life of Jesus Christ has been denied an opportunity of resonating with divine frequencies. It has always been the case that, "Where two or more of you are gathered together in my name there I am in your midst." But because of the increased population of the earth (remember it has nearly tripled just since the beginning of this century) and because of the changing subconscious climate, there are more human beings resonating today with frequencies of love and truth than ever before.

This epoch is one of those rare times in the slow rolling of the eons when lightning is able to jump down from the heavens, when the myriad and forever-turning creative cycles are all about to roll over in a row of metaphorical zeros. We are very close to the optimal moment in which a fundamental human transformation might occur, when the consciousness of eternity can wake up and come to dwell among the forms that inhabit time. You and I, our brothers and sisters, our parents, friends and co-workers are living in a moment of unprecedented historical opportunity.

A PLANETARY E E G

If it would somehow have been possible to take an EEG of the whole earth during the last hundred years and show it on a fifteen to twenty-minute run of graph paper, the resultant electromagnetic activity of the planet during this time would be seen to have a striking resemblance to the EEG of a person slowly waking from deep sleep. Almost every usable radio band is now filled with human or computer chatter of some kind; even energy spectra such as light are being tapped to facilitate human connectivity.

At what point is an awakening being considered officially awake? If it is the morning of a long-awaited occasion, such as Christmas or a wedding feast, is the individual likely to fall back asleep once the awakening is under way?

There are striking parallels between humankind and an individual mind/brain. Though many men and women of normal intelligence have been known to possess less than eight billion brain cells, the average human brain has about ten billion cells. Recent extrapolations on population growth now suggest that the earth's human population will level off around ten billion sometime during the next century.

In the human brain it is not just the number of cells, it is also very much their degree of connectivity that makes them suitable for our conscious use. It is at least coincidental to note the rapidly multiplying communication systems that connect the human family. Already, you can sit in your own home virtually anywhere on five continents and see and hear an event as it takes place on the other side of the world. As our human family is multiplying and filling every habitable corner of the earth, it is simultaneously becoming more intimate.

Though our species may be similar in some respects to a planetary brain, we will not discover our true role in relationship to the rest of the biosphere by pursuing the analogy further. Our role will only emerge as individual men and women take responsibility for establishing that most vital connectivity of all, connectivity with the incarnating wholeness of Christ's unified field of consciousness. Humanity will not need a unified field theory a century from now. By then we will have embarked upon a level of function as distinct from the historical era as waking life is distinct from sleep.

Though many ardently believe that 144,000 is the magic figure, speculation as to precisely what number of humans will be functioning in rhythmic resonance when the collective awakening is finally triggered is really beside the point. The resonant minority who will help to ground the Coming will ultimately be known only to those who compose it. While analogies and comparisons may help us to a greater awareness of the unprecedented nature of our present opportunity, the real point is to make full use of the opportunity. Healthy human bodies, minds and hearts can provide Christ with a physical means of specific action on earth. This is historically significant.

SINCE THE FALL, CHRIST HAS HAD NO SPECIFIC MEANS OF DOING ANYTHING *CONSCIOUSLY* UPON THE EARTH; HIS HANDS AND FEET HAVE BEEN TIED, CRUCIFIED BY MISPLACED HUMAN ALLEGIANCES.

Humankind is the system that Christ has designed to provide Him with a means of physical action on earth. Though Our Lord may have been directing a wonderful planetary symphony all these millennia, most of what has appeared on earth through the distorted medium of fallen human sensibilities has been chaos and discord. For brief moments there have been hints of something divine, but how soon they seem to be drowned in the noise of ignorance! All the finest and brightest moments of our racial history put together give at best but a

fleeting glimpse of our Creator's purpose. It is a purpose wonderful beyond all imaginings. To experience it as a tangible
and immediate reality, we have to be willing to play our parts.

One can hardly overstate the vital role that individuals are
designed to play. Our decision to do everything we can to offer
our bodies, minds and hearts to Christ's purposes will begin to
draw to us the tools, resources, skills and friends that will help
make our decision a living realty. Once we are connected with
the network of Christ's coordinated human family, we are in-
valuable in the individual sense; for each one of us offers our
Creator a direct doorway into human affairs.

Acupuncture has shown that a small amount of pressure on
a few seemingly isolated cells can trigger major physiological
changes throughout the entire body. In a similar way, each individual human being who enters a state of grace becomes a
sort of acupuncture point in the body of humankind. What
creative lightning might spring from Christ into the earth
through even just a few people!

Each one of us has a profound ability to communicate with
the others of our race through the collective subconscious.
There is no hocus-pocus to this; we do it all the time. Even
when we are communicating consciously with someone, our
subconscious interaction provides a major portion of our real
communication. Since all subconscious minds are intercon-
nected at a certain level, a shift at the very center of *your* being
can offer inestimable blessing into the world.

There is no telling at precisely what moment Christ may
require *only one more* healthy human being to awaken consciously into our historical time-frame. Even now, in a non-
linear sense, it is valid to say that there is only one more person required—you yourself!

THE STORY OF THE 100TH MONKEY

When a catalyst is being added to a chemical solution, there is a critical threshold where just one more molecule of the catalyst is required to trigger the desired transformation. It is not overstating the case to say that all of time and history, complete with your ancestors and all of their lives, has been just to bring *you* to this moment of realization.

Perhaps no contemporary story dramatizes the impact that a single individual can have on the collectivity of his or her species as effectively as the now famous *Story of the 100th Monkey.* When I first heard this tale, I naturally appreciated the point it was making, but I could not help wondering a bit about its authenticity. It sounded too good to be true. I did a bit of research and discovered that The 100th Monkey Story originated from the studies of a respected team of Japanese scientists. The first published account of the phenomenon appeared in an obscure 1963 scientific article by M. Kawai. The story was not brought to the attention of the American public until 1979 when Lyall Watson published an account of it in his book, *Lifetide.* From there the story spread. It has since appeared in countless books and articles. However, I have noted that a surprising number of people have yet to hear the tale. For them, I will repeat a summary of the fascinating account as it appears on pages 11 through 17 of Ken Keyes' excellent little paperback appropriately titled *The Hundredth Monkey.* If you are already acquainted with the story, feel free to skip ahead.

"The Japanese monkey, Macaca fuscata, has been observed

in the wild for a period of over 30 years. In 1952, on the island of Koshima scientists were providing monkeys with sweet potatoes dropped in the sand. The monkeys liked the taste of the raw sweet potatoes, but they found the dirt unpleasant.

"An 18-month-old female named Imo found she could solve the problem by washing the potatoes in a nearby stream. She taught this trick to her mother. Her playmates also learned this new way and they taught their mothers, too.

"This cultural innovation was gradually picked up by various monkeys before the eyes of the scientists. Between 1952 and 1958, all the young monkeys learned to wash the sandy sweet potatoes to make them more palatable. Only the adults who imitated their children learned this social improvement. Other adults kept eating the dirty sweet potatoes.

"Then something startling took place. In the autumn of 1958, a certain number of Koshima monkeys were washing sweet potatoes—the exact number is not known. Let us suppose that when the sun rose one morning there were 99 monkeys on Koshima Island who had learned to wash their sweet potatoes. Let's further suppose that later that morning, the hundredth monkey learned to wash potatoes. *Then it happened!*

"By that evening almost everyone in the tribe was washing sweet potatoes before eating them. The added energy of this hundredth monkey somehow created an ideological breakthrough!

"But notice. The most surprising thing observed by these scientists was that the habit of washing sweet potatoes then spontaneously jumped over the sea—colonies of monkeys on other islands and the mainland troop of monkeys at Takasakiyama began washing their sweet potatoes!

"Thus, when a certain critical number achieves an awareness, this new awareness may be communicated from mind to mind. Although the exact number may vary, the Hundredth Monkey Phenomenon means that when only a limited number of people know of a new way, it may remain the conscious property of these people. But there is a point at which if only one more person tunes-in to a new awareness, a

field is strengthened so that this awareness reaches everyone!''

Further commentary would be superfluous. Obviously, we
can each make a difference. Though the Father doeth the
works, individuals can make all the difference as to how,
where, and perhaps when. In each moment we face the choice
of moving either toward healthy attunement with our
Creator's purposes or toward the ever-increasing disharmonies
of those who refuse to trust in God.

If the choice were outlined for us in graphic black and
white—to either accept the qualities of God's spirit that have
been designed to express through us or to remain attuned to
suspicious, reactive habits—few of us would hesitate in
making a decision. Yet the choice in each moment is just that
clear-cut.

It could well be that much more is depending on our decision
than we might ever dare to imagine.

V

BIRTH

BORN UNDER THE STAR OF DAVID

Despite the commercialism of recent decades, the celebration of the birth of Jesus in Bethlehem nearly 2,000 years ago remains the highlight of the Western calendar. More than at any other time of year, Christmas finds a healthy and joyful spirit shared by millions of people. One has to be insensitive not to feel the intensified undercurrents of hope, peace and joy that circulate during this sacred season. People who have resigned themselves to largely unacceptable activities day after day, week after week, look up from their self-imposed hum-drum and remember that there is another way, another possibility. Even armies in open hostility will often call a twenty-four-hour cease fire when thought can turn, however briefly, to loved ones and cheerful homes.

There is a current of fresh air that circulates during the Christmas season that brings with it more than just the memory of a historical event. It is a current that carries the promise that Christ will one day return. For those with keener perception, it carries a current that says Christ is already returning through minds and hearts and spirits everywhere that are not afraid to love and receive love.

Christmas is a time when the breezes of change and renewal blow through the human heavens. "Look up!" they say. "Look up above your trivial concerns. Something is coming that will change everything. Trust in it. Meet it in the air of your own spirit. Feel it healing and blessing you; feel the descent of its peace. Share with those around you the abundance of your love and joy."

Christ is coming with a contagious joy, a communicable peace. He is awakening beneath all human consciousness, transforming everything in His path. There will be challenges, of course, for individuals beginning to attune to a whole new reality; but throughout His life, Jesus' message was that these challenges could be met victoriously. His references to persecution are often misunderstood by those who continue to imagine the Second Coming in the same terms as the first. This time it is a whole new ball game. Christ is coming in power and great glory to usher in an age of intercontinental harmony and cooperation; it will be unlike the days of old, when the new awareness was shut up and stifled. It will be a time of rejoicing and welcoming that many of the nations of the earth will be ready to receive.

The festival of Christmas reminds us that we were created to share in Christ's spirit, purpose and destiny, that there will be a time of Second Coming when Christ will return on a historically unprecedented scale. Just as the birth of Jesus in the manger at Bethlehem was the first individual Christmas, the event that many look to as the Second Coming will be the first *collective* Christmas, the time when Christ will awaken dressed in the physical bodies of an incarnate human family.

Often the dawning realization of the immensity of what is occurring is still seen through biased forms of comprehension. It is often recognized initially through the forms of understanding in an individual's consciousness most able to correlate with it. But this is fine. This is the way it needs to occur.

The Holy Spririt is working within every belief system and organization that has even a small percentage of its structure based in reality. Particularly during these next few years, it is important for us who are sharing in Christ's awakening to realize that it is not the *forms* through which our brothers and sisters are beginning to learn and understand that are important, but the *spirit* that is gradually clearing away these forms, streamlining them and making them more able to represent a direct reflection of our Creator's purpose.

It is appropriate to find the Star of David so often associated

FIGURE SIX

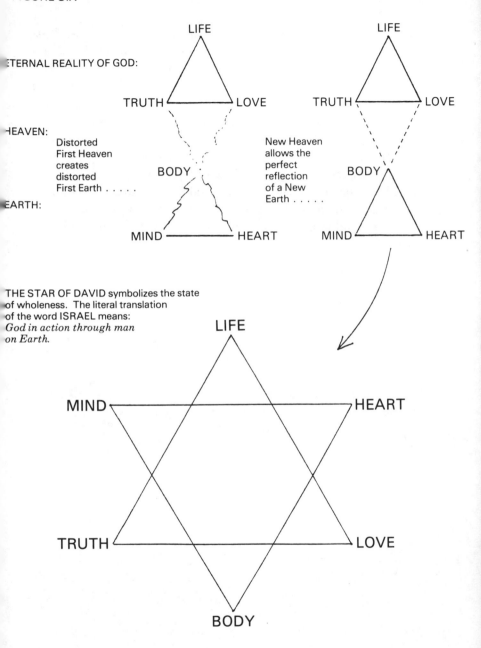

ETERNAL REALITY OF GOD:

LIFE

TRUTH — LOVE

HEAVEN:

Distorted
First Heaven
creates
distorted
First Earth . . . . .

BODY

EARTH:

MIND ——— HEART

LIFE

TRUTH — LOVE

New Heaven
allows the
perfect
reflection
of a New
Earth . . . . .

BODY

MIND — HEART

THE STAR OF DAVID symbolizes the state
of wholeness. The literal translation
of the word ISRAEL means:
*God in action through man
on Earth.*

LIFE

MIND — HEART

TRUTH — LOVE

BODY

with the Christmas season (Figure 6). It is a beautiful and fitting symbol of what is now taking place: the inverted triangle of the Creator's Spirit descending into time and matter, superimposed upon the triangle representing human beings in right polarity, drawing all matter up to God. It is fitting that such a symbol decorate the top of many a Christmas tree.

At long last, the Christmas comes, when the tree planted in the midst of the Garden, restored to a proper and creative use, can sprout the shining star. The human trinity of body, mind and heart open themselves once again to the life, universal intelligence, and love that are designed to be the source of their direction and inspiration. The Star of David becomes a living reality in a growing number of human hearts.

SOMETHING NEW UNDER THE SUN

Jesus' life and teaching on earth were a gift and example, but they were more than this: they were a point of conscious conception. Through the life of Jesus, the seeds of Christ's collective return to human consciousness were planted. There was something new under the sun, something that would take roughly two thousand years to gestate and emerge as a transformative planetary event.

The time of a child's birth is not its true beginning. By the time a child is born, it has already experienced nine months of growth and nurture in the womb. Similarly, *the historical life of Jesus coincided only with the conception of Christ in collective human consciousness.* What has been called the Second Coming represents Christ's true collective birth. Through the millennia of Christian civilization, Christ has been reorganizing the collectivity of human consciousness, drawing it, and the people associated with it, into the patterns of His soon-to-be-completed physical body. This has taken place not only in the invisible realms of heaven, but has also been reflected in the migrations and interminglings of the earth's human population throughout this last 2,000 year period. Though the fetus may be unaware of the purpose behind its various body parts, these parts continue to develop nevertheless.

THE PHYSICAL PLANE IS THE MANGER WHERE CHRIST IS TO BE BORN. HUMAN BEINGS ATTUNED TO GOD'S PURPOSES WILL COMPOSE THE BODY OF THE CHRIST CHILD.

During what we have referred to as a collective gestation process, *Homo sapiens* have been enfolded in the heavy materialistic womb of the earth's gravity. Because we have disregarded the Creator's initial instructions, we have been conscious during this period in a way in which we were not intended to be conscious until after birth. Consequently we have experienced fear and self-imposed pain. However, be that as it may, the gestation has not been caused to abort; it has just become more difficult for the kind of identities that human beings have assumed.

Before emerging into the world at birth, the human fetus gestates in the womb for 280 days. Instead of 280 *terrestrial* days, suppose that it took 280 *solar* days *on each of the seven frequencies* of universal manifestation for Christ's consciousness to reach a level of full activity. If this were the case, by the year 1680 A.D. Christ would have awakened on six of the seven frequencies. If we add to this the 33 years of Jesus' earthly life, we find ourselves at the beginning of the eighteenth century industrial revolution. The coarsest of the seven channels of creative manifestation, and the last to be penetrated, would naturally be the physical. A gestation of 280 solar days on each of the seven frequencies would take 1960 years. If we add to that, 33 years and make adjustments for the discrepancies of the early calendar, we find that there is something to be said for the closing years of the Twentieth Century that few other ages could claim.

Through the life of Jesus, the Creator stitches the thread of truth deeply into a fallen race. And then Jesus ascends with the words, "I go unto the Father to prepare a place for you." Still in human form, the ascended Christ brings the news of our fallen predicament to the attention of the highest, subtlest levels of universal awareness. He secures their assistance and moves on, spending the next 1960 years doing the same: weaving in and out of every level of creative manifestation, establishing the conditions that will make His collective birth on earth sustainable for all eternity.

Though it is best to regard all such cyclical analysis figuratively, there is one more that we might note in passing.

The Mayan Indians of Central America saw time flowing in millennia-long, cyclical tides. According to their calculations, the last great cosmic tide went out in 3114 B.C. and is due to return, bringing with it a new age of the gods, in 2011 A.D. **The Mayan calendar pinpointed the years between 1987 and 2011** as difficult years, accompanying the end of what they called "The Age of Chaos."

There is an unmistakable sense of something sacred about to happen here on this earth. The image is of a woman, nine months pregnant with child. Human attitudes and activities cannot affect the inevitability of the birth, but they can help to determine whether humankind experiences the birth as natural or apocalyptic. There may be some inevitable contractions felt through tightening monetary policies or through rapid adjustments of one sort or another. But just as the human mother continues to breathe easily and deeply throughout the contractions of natural childbirth, so those who are consciously helping to prepare the way of the Lord breathe easily, trusting throughout these times of transition that what is occurring is not only inevitable, but precisely what we have been longing for.

THE MANGER OF HERE AND NOW

So many seek Christ hither and yon. Others remain forever in preparation, always looking to the future. There is nothing wrong with preparation—provided it comes to an end! There is nothing wrong with a doorway—*provided* one makes use of it and walks on through. As C. S. Lewis once pointed out, the practice of Christianity in the civilized world has been one of people climbing up a signpost instead of following the road that it indicates.

Christ's historical birth in Bethlehem was a vital point of conception for the human race. But it cannot be worshipped as a tame and antiquated event. Christmas is a reminder to welcome Christ's birth today, in this very moment. It is a reminder to open our minds to a universal awareness and our hearts to an eternal love.

What does it mean to accept Christ? Firstly, that we present ourselves and all that we are before the Lord. We do not wait until we are "ready" or until our lives are "more presentable." We offer our incompletion into the fields of divine energy, to be restructured by the only hands that can shape us in the image and likeness of our inherent truth. To accept Christ is to work with the very next step in front of us, to rejoice in the immediate situation at hand, to accept our circumstances for what they are and to introduce healing.

How many would-be agents of creative reconstruction (Figure 7) render their good intentions impotent by cursing and blaming their immediate situation? Instead of accepting Christ and allowing something potent to transform their worlds, they hesitate year after year, always waiting for the

THE FALL OF THE WOULD-BE HEALER.

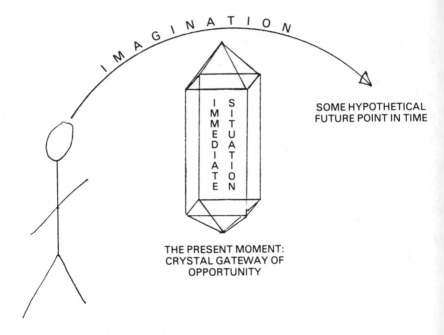

IMAGINATION

IMMEDIATE SITUATION

SOME HYPOTHETICAL
FUTURE POINT IN TIME

THE PRESENT MOMENT:
CRYSTAL GATEWAY OF
OPPORTUNITY

The would-be healer is always getting it together, always postponing
the moment of transformation until idealized conditions are fulfilled.

ideal situation. This is just the same Old Adam and Eve consciousness hiding behind the trees of the garden.

Many know that transformation is possible, perhaps even likely, but they have not yet arranged their material circumstances the way they want them to be when they finally allow the change to come. What if that had been the attitude of Mary and Joseph? With beautiful humility and noble grace, they accepted their situation precisely as it was. Christ was born in a manger.

To truly accept Christ's freedom, we must first accept ourselves, not making a great issue out of either our successes or our failures, but stepping in perfect trust, just as we are, into the creative fires. Christ's consciousness is a gift for all to share. It is not to be hidden away (in the Inn) where only the privileged few shall have access to it. It is to emerge out in the open where kings and shepherds, wise men, beggars, animals and angels alike can all revel together in its wonder and majesty.

When we withhold Christ's transformative love from our immediate situation, while with good intentions trying to arrange things in some way that we feel would be more suitable, we prevent the birth of Christ in the here and now of a personal world that greatly requires Him.

We each have emotions that color our expression. They share the manger of our body consciousness. We do not have to be ashamed of them. We present them to the Lord just as they are; *this is the only way they are tamed and brought into right relationship with the rest of our lives.* Many spend years repressing their passions in some imagined form of spiritual growth, always unsuccessfully trying to eradicate them from daily behavior, never realizing that these very feelings are like the beasts of the manger. When the Presence of the living Christ is born into their midst, they become useful raw material for a transformed identity.

OUR IMMEDIATE HERE AND NOW SITUATION IS THE MANGER INTO WHICH CHRIST LONGS TO BE BORN.

It is the doorway, the portal, the vortex through which the

flood of Christ's reality will enter our world. Through the symbolic configuration of our immediate personal circumstance, we are each in touch with all the world's ills. When we allow Christ to enter our lives, complete with all their imperfections, we give the Creator the opportunity to heal the world through the symbolism of our seemingly personal events. Each of us has habitual modes of behavior that correlate with basic patterns of malfunction in collective behavior.

As long as we jump over the immediate situation at hand, cursing it, blaming it, saying, "If only it were different . . . , " we remain part of the problem. In such a case, it will make little difference what we profess or desire, we will not be part of the solution.

There are seasons for right changes, but if we seek change because we have refused to accept the challenges and opportunities of our present situation, we offer nothing to life's purpose and we play no meaningful role in planetary healing.

So often we imagine Christ as the miracle worker who walked on water, cured the blind, and raised the dead in spirit. We forget that He ate breakfast, washed His clothes, and worked with the tools of a carpentry trade. We forget that He had parents, relatives and friends and no doubt dealt with the entire range of day-to-day activities that each of us faces. Perhaps it was here in the little things of moment-by-moment living that Christ's most meaningful miracles occurred.

Our circumstance now, as it is in this very moment, complete with its imperfections, is where we have been planted; it is where we are intended to bloom. It is here that we have the ability to offer the greatest blessing into the momentous affairs of our times.

THE "SINNER" COP-OUT

Accepting Christ into our lives draws out the potential of both ourselves and our immediate world. It actualizes *the next step* for us, whatever that next step needs to be. The next step for one is not necessarily the next step for another. We do not demand that others put on *our* image of what *we think* Christ should be, anymore than we ourselves conform to some human image.

Often the emergence of Spirit that could take place in a group of awakening friends is limited by the subtle demands that they place on one another. It is prudent to "judge not." We are all equally essential parts of our Creator's developing earthly body; but we are not equal in the sense that we each need to experience Christ in identical terms. For one person the next step may be to begin speaking more. For another, the next step may be to listen more and speak less.

During this season when the last tatters of limited human understanding are being blown away in the clarification of the new spiritual era, we can greatly assist the process by confining our judgments (if we must judge) to the realm for which we are responsible, the realm of our immediate body, mind and heart. Even here, in the immediate neighborhood of self, it is important not to institutionalize our failures by judging ourselves too harshly.

Exaggerated repentance is a reversed form of pride.

We are designed to acknowledge our imbalances, adjust for them *and move on.* Accepting forgiveness in every moment in which it is required, letting go of yesterday's failures, we move forward in healing. Clinging to images of ourselves as sinners hinders the healing process. It is the fall of many a would-be Christian. Nothing can be gained by locking oneself into an image of failure. All have been sinners. Everyone has in some way contributed to the fallen world. But wallowing in the image of a sinner never got anyone to heaven. If there was one message that Christ repeatedly strove to get across it was that *we* are not sinners, that that is not where our primary identity should lie.

> Is it not written in your law, I said, Ye are gods?
>
> John 10: 34

> Ye are the light of the world.
>
> Matthew 5: 14

> Verily, verily I say unto you, He that believeth in me, the works that I do shall he do also; and greater works than these shall he do
> . . .
>
> John 14: 12

> Be ye therefore perfect, even as your Father which is in heaven is perfect.
>
> Matthew 5: 48

Thinking of ourselves in terms of failure does not offer Christ much to work with. It is vital to acknowledge our failures, but only in order to correct them and move on. The acknowledgement need only be a brief perception and adjustment. There is nothing that could ever prevent us from receiving God's forgiveness, except perhaps our own refusal to accept it. Once we are forgiven, we experience an identity with its roots in Christ's living spirit. We come to understand ourselves in the image and likeness of Him who calls us into being. Needless to say, it is a positive image.

The Creator is interested in neither grovelling sinners nor arrogant idolaters. He is interested in men and women of integrity who are willing to accept themselves as awakening, historical creatures.

Our essential spirit is like a graceful silver bird flying through the polluted skies of fallen consciousness. As this being of light flies through the smoggy atmosphere of disintegrating human illusions, it collects some residue on its wings. Occasionally we stop to clean off our wings, to scrape off the residue that we have picked up in the foggy skies of earth. As we have the humility to acknowledge and release our failures, we come to see the distinction. *We* are not the residue that may have collected on our wings. *We* are something eternal, organizing our field of awareness to reflect increasingly the image and likeness of God.

Our processes of healing will show us failures; we must see where we are going before we can adjust the course. However, *the healing process does not define us!* It is just the manner in which we awaken. It is vital to recognize the false pride of the sinner for what it is: a cop-out, an escape mechanism through which the fearful avoid responsibility—and, as they eventually find out, salvation.

BEHOLD, I MAKE ALL THINGS NEW

In the early days of the earth there was no soil or vegetation, only cooling rocks, clay and ocean. Do you suppose the first cells had hints of a coming biosphere teeming with untold billions of organic life-forms? Do you suppose they had premonitions of the coming supertapestry of biological earth reaching for the sun? Perhaps such intuitive premonitions in these early cells helps to account for their incredible enthusiasm and indomitable will to multiply and cover the earth.

The awakening of humankind is to the rest of the universe what the stirring of the first single-celled creature was to the biosphere of the earth. Should we ever be tempted by discouragement, the prospect of universal exploration as conscious members of the Creator's own temporal exploratory team should certainly serve to inspire us. The joy of it all! The vision of it! The amazing universal architect behind this beneficent arrangement and design!

We are not misplaced shoots in some forgotten garden, but the harvest of a long awaited season that was initiated when the world was young. We belong in the Creator's garden. Not one of us that shows promise of bearing fruit will be neglected or uncared for. It may appear that we have to struggle against resisting cultural tendencies, but do not be misled by appearances. If we keep our trust in God and walk on to meet them, all seeming obstacles will dissolve in our path. And the worse their initial appearance, the more they will help us along our way. In this age, faith is a short-term strategy, soon rewarded in the certainty of divine experience.

"Behold, I make all things new," the spirit assures. So it is for ourselves and for our worlds as we abide close to the core of the ascending flame of Christ's eternal love and allow our hearts to be purified. We are similar to moths fluttering around a candle flame, only in our case our highest destiny is to merge in union with the flame, not to singe our wings, but to find them for the first time.

Union with Christ proves to be union with all living things. It implies communion and community. Union. Communion. Community. Three words with the same root that flow into one another like the singularity of Christ's being flowing into a healthy human family. As we grow in spirit, we find that the lives of others are joined with ours. Separate in an individual sense, but one with us motivationally and spiritually, we experience friends and co-workers in an intimate way. Like fingers on the same hand or notes in a single chord, we work together, sharing a common purpose, honoring a common vision.

When two or more are functioning together in such a way, the dynamic principle of union, synthesis and fusion begins working in their midsts. This is how activity in Christ's name is amplified: through the same principle of *fusion* that fuels the fiery passion of the sun and burns in the heart of every star.

In nuclear *fission*, energy is produced by breaking apart the bonds that hold matter together. But in nuclear *fusion*, energy is produced by forming new bonds, bringing additional matter into newer, dynamic intimate relationship. This is the way the sun creates energy and light. This same principle of fusion characterizes the nature of the growing groups of awakening human spirits. It is this force of cohesion, blending, bringing together in spirit, communion and community, that allows the coming birth to be easy and natural.

And so it is that time passes and the world is fulfilled.

Into the childlike consciousness of a restored humankind, Christ is born upon this third planet from the star we call Sun. There is a new reality on Terra's soil: the third, the unprecedented, the promise, the fulfillment.

Glory to God in the highest and on earth, peace to all creatures of goodwill; for in this day all goodwills blend into One God's will. Christ is born. The veil that has divided heaven and earth is dissolved.

VI

HEALING

HEALING IN HEAVEN

The first step into dimensional expression occurs in heaven. In a realm of divine ideation, all things are born initially as ideas. They come into existence first as invisible fields of energy. Only later is matter drawn into their spheres of influence, providing them with visible form.

The most pragmatic of all the sciences, physics itself, has recently discovered this to be the case. Many of those now working at its frontiers have found the existence of "heaven" to be such a vital part of their work that they have labeled it with various terms. English physicist David Bohm refers to it as the "implicate order." He speaks of "a geometrical substrata of pure form in essence." This is one description of the Kingdom of Heaven.

The perfect patterns exist vibrationally all around us. God's heaven interpenetrates the earth. God's will is done in heaven. The fact that God's will is not being done on earth as it is in heaven, indicates that something is distorting the natural processes that should be allowing God's will to be reflected on earth.

Fearful thought, taking place in the "heaven" of human consciousness, distorts the way God's heaven manifests on earth. It is here, in a sort of false heaven, or *first heaven* that the designs originating in universal intelligence become distorted. We can refer to this as *the first heaven* because this is the *first part of heaven* to touch human consciousness. It is the heaven that immediately surrounds human beings, the heaven of our personal, as well as our collective, thought. This distorted first heaven creates a distorted earth. As John points out in Revelation 21: 1-8, the first heaven must pass away.

> And I saw a new heaven and a new earth: for the first heaven and the first earth were passed away: and there was no more sea.

> Revelation 21: 1

There was no more sea of separation between God and Man. "And I John saw the holy city . . . "
The word *city* here refers to a state of consciousness.

> And I John saw the holy city, New Jerusalem, coming down from God out of heaven, prepared as a bride adorned for her husband.

> Revelation 21: 2

This holy state of consciousness, offered to God by a whole and healed humanity, is in right polarity. It is the bride of Christ. Its feminine or receptive face is turned toward the truth that is coming into form out of the new heaven.

> And I heard a great voice out of heaven saying, Behold the tabernacle of God is with men, and he will dwell with them, and they shall be his people, and God himself shall be with them, and be their God.

> Revelation 21: 3

When humanity returns to proper polarity, God's will is done on earth as it is in heaven.

> And God shall wipe away all tears from their eyes; and there shall be no more death, neither sorrow, nor crying, neither shall there be any more pain . . .

> Revelation 21: 4

None of these things are God's will.

> . . . for the former things are passed away. And he that sat upon the throne said, Behold, I

make all things new ... I am Alpha and
Omega, the beginning and the end. I will give
unto him that is athirst of the fountain of the
water of Life freely. He that overcometh shall
inherit all things; and I will be his God, and he
shall be my son.

Revelation 21: 4,5,6,7,

When the receptive face of human consciousness is turned
toward the Creator, perceiving His designs in heaven, the active face of humanity is helping those designs of heaven come
into form on earth. Then Christ is present. There are no
problems.

Christ is already present *in heaven*, but He is not yet consciously incarnate in a responsive human family. Since the
polarity reversal, the receptive face of humanity has been
looking for external direction from the environment round
about. The active face of humanity has been busy creating in
heaven.

Instead of listening to God and acting on earth, humankind
has historically listened for direction to evolving processes.
The result has been that human creative activity, instead of
producing beauty on earth, has produced a proliferation of ill
spirits in the first heaven. This is backwards. It was never intended that human beings create spirits. And it was never intended that incomplete evolutionary processes determine
human behavior.

Just as God created the heaven before he created the earth,
so in *re-creation*, the first heaven needs to pass away before
divine processes can freely operate once again. Something in
our own consciousness needs to change before our efforts at
healing the earth will succeed. The physician must first address him or herself.

AN EXERCISE

There comes a time in each healing process when one begins to recognize the presence of two distinct modes of consciousness. Each of these perceives and interprets experience differently. Each has its own way of operating and its own way of approaching decision-making. Each is based in a sense of self. One sense of self is spiritual and is designed to be primary, the other is associated with the individual body and is designed to be secondary. The body consciousness, or *ego*, is based on the tangible, the immediate and the sensory; the spirit consciousness is based on purpose, intention and vision. The ego is designed to play a supportive role to the spirit.

The healing process sorts out the intermingling of these two selves and places spirit clearly in charge. It helps individuals learn of the two natures within them and the right use of each.

The ego has a set of values that are designed to care for the physical body and protect it from harm. When it is allowed to control decision-making, the ego is overcautious in the extreme; dangers and possible threats become exaggerated; and the individual often finds him or herself functioning out of fear.

Yet the ego does not have to die as some believe; it has only to become transformed from a dictator into a servant, from the absolute monarch of consciousness into a friend and helper. In a healthy state, its perspectives remain to modify behavior, but behavior is initiated by spirit.

A simple exercise which helps to distinguish more clearly between spirit and ego is to outline one's long-term, lifetime priorities. Most people are vaguely aware of these. It is often not until they outline them on paper that these priorities come fully to awareness. Once one has defined one's life purposes, it becomes easier to see which decisions lead to action that supports these purposes and which decisions lead to action that hinders these purposes.

The exercise of writing out a list of soul purposes can be expanded to include a list of all your activities. Next to each of these activities, write what you honestly recognize as your root motivation. You will discover which of your habitual activities are motivated by love (springing from spirit) and which are motivated by fear (springing from ego). When you find some habitual activity springing from a fear of some sort, you will want to examine into it.

More than any other single factor, fear keeps people locked in unsatisfying behavior. The stress that results from this lies at the root of disease. If we are interested in addressing the root causes of disease and returning to spirit-motivated behavior, we need to look boldly at our fears.

The ego will often present fear in a guise of responsible concern, making it appear logical and reasonable. But fear is fear; the body always knows the difference. No matter how convincingly the ego may justify fear, the body that has to live with it will not be healthy. Fear is designed to play only a minuscule role in a healthy life.

On those few occasions when fear serves some useful purpose, its appearance is brief and to the point.

The useful and protective appearance of fear is more aptly called *fright*. Fright is what one may feel on a street corner at the sudden approach of an automobile. It may cause one to jump back and so save the body from damage. However, *fright has only momentary usefulness*. It was never intended to be a permanent state of existence.

In our modern world, fright has become institutionalized under a thousand and one poorly-understood brands of subliminal anxiety. This is a devastating condition, robbing us of vitality, awareness and good health. Becoming aware of our anxieties is the first step toward removing their subliminal influence from our lives.

When we take time to address the roots of our anxieties, we find that they invariably fall into one of three categories.

The first and by far the largest category into which anxieties fall, could be simply labeled *the irrational.* These anxieties are often concerned with basic survival issues that the ego has blown out of proportion. They are warning of physical dangers that are statistically improbable, if not downright impossible. Once these anxieties are understood, they can be dismissed *en masse.* They are thoroughly irrelevant: *F*alse *E*vidence *A*ppearing *R*eal.

The second category of anxiety stems from what appear as possibilities, but possibilities *beyond conscious control.* The threat of imminent nuclear disaster or the threat of a potential heart attack may lie at the root of anxieties in this category. Once we have done what we can about these issues, whether that implies political action or sufficient exercise, we need to totally release the fear of what conceivably *might* result from circumstances beyond our control; it is illogical and counter-productive to maintain anxiety. Once we have taken the requisite action, we trust in God to take care of the rest.

The third category of anxiety is *fright ignored,* valid sensings disregarded. Anxieties in this category stem from an awareness of impending danger that we have refused to look at and deal with adequately. The body consciousness of a smoker may be telling him or her that smoking is causing serious respiratory damage, that the first stages of cancer are appearing. This is a useful form of fear, urging an immediate change of habit in order to preserve the ability of the body to host life. Immediate action is required to sustain a state of well being. But once the action has been initiated, the fear should be turned off. It is like a doorbell or a warning light; it need only be present briefly to alert us to the needed change.

Fear is a parasite, sapping vitality, destroying health, and diminishing consciousness. We do not need to accept it as a part of our lives. Subconscious fears will remain to trouble us so long as they are repressed or ignored; their only exit point is through the conscious mind. Taking time out to look at our fears, inviting them up out of the subconscious realm into the light of day, may not be a particularly enjoyable exercise, but it is necessary if we are to return to healthy, spirit-motivated function.

SATAN

Satan is a creation of fallen human consciousness. He is energized by human fear. Since all human beings share a collective spirit, the fear that people channel into Satan allows him to exert an influence of fear upon all our race. However, we do not need to fear Satan. God has given us the authority to put him in his place. We need to use that authority to dismiss him firmly from our conscious affairs.

Prior to the Fall, Satan did not exist in the detrimental capacity in which he now serves. Still, the stuff of which he is made did exist. It has a rightful place. Satan is to collective human consciousness precisely what the body consciousness is to the individual. Satan is our collective ego.

Satan does not need to be destroyed or abolished; he needs only to be taught to follow behind us, as a shadow. A shadow is useful only in its place. When we determine our behavior on the basis of what our shadow appears to be doing, we are caught in a closed system, under the influence of effects; we are bound to get into trouble.

Satan was designed to be kept in a subconscious environment. He is the guardian of the past. He is the keeper of our files and records, our patterns and memories. In that capacity, and in that capacity alone, Satan serves our race well. His nature on his native turf is to complement our creative intentions, not to thwart them. However, when Satan's influence is allowed to escape the subconscious realms, his impact on human consciousness is devastating. It leads to misery, decay, suffering and death. Satan is not doing this because he is "bad." This is just the effect of a fear-rooted nature that is out of place in human awareness.

When fire destroys a forest, we do not say the fire is "bad." We have better sense. We use fire every day of our lives and are thankful for its nature being what it is. The same is true of Satan. So long as human beings (through ignorance) invite Satan into their consciousness, he will destroy all that he encounters there. When invited, he does what he was designed to do: he limits, curtails, defines, judges, and constricts. Satan's characteristics are *limitation, curtailment, definition, judgment* and *constriction*. These characteristics are essential components of a healthy creation, however, in the realms of human consciousness they were intended to be *conscious prerogatives*. Satan bandies them about willy-nilly.

Satan is not happy with his unrestrained freedom in human affairs. He longs to be put in his place just as the ego of each human being longs to meet its spiritual master. Satan, like any creature of God, is happiest and most useful in his natural habitat. When he met Jesus in the wilderness, Satan was not seeking to destroy Christ. He was exercising his nature to ascertain if Christ was indeed the Son of God who had for so long been absent from human consciousness. Satan must have been not unpleasantly surprised with Christ's authoritative rebuke. You may have noticed, he willingly obeyed the Lord's command.

After the three temptations, there is no further record of Satan troubling Christ. He had met his master and proved to his own satisfaction that this indeed was He whom he was designed to serve. Not only did Satan obey Christ's initial order and cease to trouble Jesus further, he required his legions of ill spirits to do likewise.

As we reassume our Christ nature in the course of awakening, we will each encounter Satan. Before we can dismiss him from our consciousness, we must learn to recognize his presence. As the Holy Spirit begins working in our lives, we begin to see Satan more distinctly. We begin to recognize his habitual realm of input. We discover that though he packages his logic in a multitude of ways, essentially, he has only three basic approaches.

SATAN AND THE HOLY CITY

Christ was successfully able to put Satan in his place largely because Christ recognized that this was indeed Satan speaking to Him. Many others have heard this same logic and have simply assumed it was the voice of reason or common sense.

One day you are likely to find yourself in an encounter similar to the one experienced by Jesus after his 40 days in the desert. Satan will come to you with one form or another of his *Model A approach.* He says, "Look, friend, you need a lot of support-systems to keep you alive on the physical plane. You need food, clothing, shelter and the cash to supply these things. In a word, you need bread. You need basic physical sustenance. 'If thou be the son of God, command that these stones be made into bread.'" Stones? What is the stone?

The stone is the heart that harbors fear. In the fallen state, the heart has been holding itself in stony patterns, initiating behavior in fear to provide for the exaggerated security needs of the ego. Satan encourages this. He suggests that concern, anxiety, and behavior springing out of fear (of inadequate food, clothing and shelter) is the best way to ensure survival. In the fallen state, the ego is susceptible to such logic.

As long as the ego does not meet its spiritual master-self, it is fundamentally afraid. It is like a child out on a hike with an experienced guide, suddenly finding herself alone. Such a child knows that her security lies in the guide's wisdom and overview, but the guide is nowhere to be found. The ego does its best to run the affairs of the fallen man or woman, but it is so fearful and its defenses are so elaborate, that it inadvertently keeps out the spiritual master-self for whom it secretly longs.

What Satan was ascertaining in the First Temptation was how Christ, functioning without fear, would be able to survive on the physical plane. The First Temptation clarified the distinction between spirit and ego, between Christ and Satan, so that both could enter a relationship where Christ was clearly dominant and Satan was clearly subservient. Christ speaks to his material nature saying in effect, "No, of course I won't make bread out of my fears. Fear is not a viable way to pursue material needs. Besides, Satan, you are not even sure any longer just what humankind's true needs are. 'It is written, Man shall not live by bread alone, but by every word that proceedeth out of the mouth of God.' "

Christ met the first temptation and rejected the assault of fear-motivation on a primal level within himself. As He did this He established a pattern*, a prototype, a blueprint for all to follow. More importantly, He represented every one of us within the collective consciousness of our entire species and broke through a certain crust or barrier, rendering it easier ever after for others to do the same.

On the archetypal level where the encounter between Christ and Satan takes place, individual and collective are one. Christ's stance is an eternal shield against temptation, a shield that is available to each one of us to hold forth whenever fear would urge us to make bread of stone.

In the Second Temptation, Satan tries to push Christ a little farther in the direction that Christ is already going. Many of us are aware of how this technique has been politically applied. If a movement or some growing influence is perceived as threatening, vested interests will often infiltrate it, donate money to it, stimulate it, encourage it and expose it to excessive media coverage. Usually the individuals within the movement, unaware of what is happening, welcome the sudden interest. If they remain unaware, they are manipulated into

---

* What physicist Rupert Sheldrake would call a *morphogenetic field.*

premature and poorly timed action. In this way, what might have been much more difficult to oppose or terminate *from without* is rendered impotent *from within.* In the Second Temptation, Satan seeks to push Jesus just a little bit farther along *good* lines, along the positive lines of thought that Jesus employs in His spirit-motivated behavior.

> Then the devil taketh him up into the holy city, and setteth him on a pinnacle of the temple. And saith unto him, If thou be the Son of God, cast thyself down: for it is written, He shall give his angels charge concerning thee: and in their hands they shall bear thee up, lest at any time thou dash thy foot against a stone.
>
> Matthew 4: 5-6

Eventually Satan comes to each of us with this *Model B approach.* We have already met the First Temptation successfully, so he tries to use the momentum of our victory to his advantage:

"Well, my friend, you may be right I suppose. You seem to be able to meet your survival needs without me. I've noticed you seem to be doing quite well without worry or concern. You have done it. Congratulations. I no longer detect any fear in your decision-making processes. It is obvious that you don't need to worry. Go ahead. Become arrogant. Don't bother to respect common sense at all. You have seen miracles happen. God is unlimited. Your good behavior has brought you up into the holy city itself. You are in a very positive state of consciousness. You already share in God's assurance. You know the spirit is working through you. Relax. Be careless. Get sloppy. Let the little things slide. No need to pay attention to detail. Not only are you in the holy city now, you are on the **very pinnacle of the temple. You have walked back into the control room. You have taken charge of your mind/brain cir**cuitry for the first time in ages. You see all the things that are possible to you as incarnate spirit, all the things which you are **likely to do here in time and space. Go ahead. I dare you. Disregard me completely. Why, you don't even need me in** your subconscious. You don't need any common sense at all. Cast thyself down. Your angels will protect you. It is written that they will not even let you dash your foot against a stone."

Fortunately Christ knew better. He knew who Satan was. He did not want to disregard him completely. He wanted him to continue in his subconscious responsibilities. Jesus knew that while material caution and basic common sense were always to remain on board as advisors, influencing the *style* of behavior, they were to never at any time dictate what that behavior should be as Satan was now attempting to do.

"It is written again," Christ replied, "Thow shalt not tempt the Lord thy God."

In successfully meeting the Second Temptation, Jesus established His authority in a realm of consciousness where Satan had held sway since the Fall.

The three temptations symbolize three tests that await those who awaken in Christ. They encapsulate the three basic fear-rooted processes of logic that perpetuate the fallen state. Each temptation occurs on a level more subtle than the last.

The First Temptation can be couched in a thousand terms, but essentially it can be summed up by labeling it *Fear for Physical Survival.* The Second Temptation represents the other extreme: *A Lack of Commonsensical Respect for the Nature of the Physical Plane.* The Third Temptation gets right to the root of the first two and addresses *Self-Reflection* itself.

THE LAST TEMPTATION

In the created realms, the Creator knows Himself through a process of self-reflection that includes others. Healthy consciousness does not reflect directly upon itself. There are supposed to be intermediary life-forms that represent aspects of consciousness to other aspects of consciousness. If we are to share the Creator's nature, we must appreciate His attitude toward self-reflection.

When consciousness reflects upon its own self-awareness, the entity gets involved in feedback. Its perception is distorted by a subjective evaluation of good and evil. The nature of the forbidden fruit is such that roughly half of the time this results in chaos, fear and disease. Since the self-reflective organism can handle only so much disease, its life-span becomes limited.

In the Third Temptation, Satan tried to get Christ to make an intellectual, rather than a spiritual decision. This is precisely what was forbidden in the garden. The conscious mind is not supposed to be running feasibility studies and anticipating future events based on past experiences as they appear in its own conceptual analysis. This is not how behavior is determined in a healthy state.

> Again, the devil taketh him up into an exceeding high mountain, and sheweth him all the kingdoms of the world, and the glory of them; And saith unto him, All these things will I give thee, if thou wilt fall down and worship

me. Then saith Jesus unto him, Get thee
hence, Satan, for it is written, Thou shalt worship the Lord thy God, and him only shalt thou
serve.

Matthew 4: 8-10

"All these things" that the devil would give unto Jesus
belonged to Jesus anyway. The devil was only presuming to
have authority in the matter. He had finally sensed what he
thought to be a loophole. For the interval of Satan's influence,
Christ found Himself looking at the future. He saw all the
kingdoms of the world as they would be one day after the
Great Healing was complete, all responding to His nature.

Satan was asking Jesus to look at the likely implications of
the successful completion of His work, all the great good that
He would accomplish. He was asking Jesus to motivate Himself *in order to see a certain goal accomplished,* rather than
simply allowing achievement to occur as He proceeded a step
at a time. This is Satan's *Model C approach.* He was attempting to get Jesus to reflect upon Himself and His probable effects on earth in a fallen pattern of self-reflection. Jesus knew
that this would amount to worshipping an image of Himself,
rather than the reality of His Father's Spirit. He did not buy
it.

Get thee hence, Satan, for it is written Thou
shalt worship the Lord thy God and Him only
shalt thou serve.

Matthew 4: 10

In successfully meeting this Third and last Temptation,
Jesus clearly defined the relationship between His Spirit and
His material nature. He left no doubt of His spiritual
authority. Satan, the ego, is banished from consciousness,
directed hence, ordered to return to the realm where he
belongs.

OVERLAPPING ENERGY NETWORKS

Since the time when human beings began allowing their behavior to be determined by the external environment, a large percentage of the animating current available to them has been mischanneled into fear and behavior motivated by fear. The consciousness field around the earth, which was designed to carry a powerful expansive love charge, became polluted with an energy network of fear. The energy network of God's love continued to draw out the divine potential of developing humankind on subconscious levels, but on most conscious frequencies it was no longer able to get through. The network of fear began to dominate human relationship.

The humanly created network of fear is but a thin film on a veritable ocean of love-centered events and processes. Nevertheless, it is sufficient to distort the surface of human awareness, cutting off a *conscious* connection between Creator and creation.

During what we have called the gestation of humanity, human beings with lives rooted in fear have been allowed to multiply. But this arrangement was never intended to last forever. Jesus describes the coming of the Kingdom of Heaven through the parable of the weeds growing in among the wheat. He concludes the parable by saying:

> Let both (wheat and weeds) grow together until the harvest: and in the time of harvest I will say to the reapers, Gather ye together first the tares and bind them in bundles to burn them: but gather the wheat into my barn.
>
> Matthew 13: 30

This parable, and the coming event to which it pertains, is one of the key teachings that distinguishes Christianity from the other religions of the world. Repeatedly throughout His life, Jesus pointed to a certain separation phenomenon, a coming event that, curiously, is ignored by both the religions of the East and the philosophies of the West. Jesus spoke of a time when the vibrational frequencies of fear that have been overlapping the vibrational frequencies of love, would be removed from the atmosphere of this planet. This will be a historically unprecedented event. The philosophies of both East and West have resigned themselves to the acceptance of evil as a necessary shadow of good. As far as I know, none of them has addressed the following three possibilities:

> * That *fear* might lie at the root of all that humans deem to be evil.

> * That fear might be associated with an actual frequency of the matter/energy continuum.

> * That it is theoretically possible to prevent this fear frequency from influencing the earth and its occupants.

In much the same way that the ozone absorbs certain radiation before it reaches the earth, a change in the emotional condition of human beings could create a climate where *fear* would not be taken seriously. The fact that this would at some point occur was stressed by Jesus through a number of parables. The removal of the fear frequencies is the sword that Jesus warned would precede the peace.

There are apocalyptic as well as transformative implications.

NOT PEACE, BUT DIVISION

At the time of Christ's victory over control by the external environment, a separation process was initiated in the collective subconscious of humankind, a separation between the overlapping energy networks of love and fear. This process of separation has been gradually becoming more conscious during the two millennia since Christ's Ascension. The detonation of the first nuclear device in 1945 marked the beginning of this separation process on conscious levels. Since the close of World War II, human beings have been living under new conditions of consciousness. The days of judgment are under way.

THE TIMES IN WHICH WE ARE LIVING ARE CHARACTERIZED BY *THE POLARIZATION OF LOVE AND FEAR.*

We might compare the contents of human consciousness to an equal mixture of sand and iron filings. The sand represents the habits, behavioral patterns, beliefs, etc. that are rooted in fear. The iron filings represent the structures that are rooted in love. Historically, they have been thoroughly mixed. They have been mixed in every race, tribe, nation and individual.

As Christ comes, all the love elements of human consciousness are drawn up into the love networks of His being and all the fear elements are repelled into subconscious levels. Christ lifts the love-centered up out of the love/fear mixture just as a magnet would lift iron filings.

> And I, if I be lifted up from the earth, will
> draw all men unto me.

John 12: 32

Christ is coming to bring peace to the earth. But the only way to achieve a *sustainable* peace is to remove the energy network of fear that has been sapping the vitality of humankind. Christ comes first with the great sword of division, the Last Judgment, that will sort all elements into their proper places.

> Suppose ye that I am come to give peace on
> earth? I tell you, Nay; but rather division:

Luke 12: 51

Christ's presence clears the consciousness field surrounding the earth so that the creations of the true heaven might manifest undistorted. The separation has not occurred sooner because Christ wanted to first restructure the subconscious realm in a way that would provide a safety net for human beings during the separation process. He wanted to give human beings immersed in the fear network every possible chance of surviving its removal.

The Mormons have a painting which depicts the Coming of Christ in a cloud of glory. As the cloud of Christ's presence engulfs the earth, people are depicted within the cloud rejoicing at the transformative presence of their healer and Lord. But at the edges of the cloud, outside the cloud, other people are shown choking and gagging, reacting to the cloud as if it were tear gas.

The same event, the same presence, the same intensification of spirit brings salvation to some, exile to others.

Currently, the most tangible evidence of the separation process lies in the increasing polarization between love-motivated and fear-motivated people. The close of World War II saw a thorough mixture of love and fear in most people. However, since then people are tending to favor one *modus operandi* or the other.

The 1980's find may more people who are either *predominantly* love-motivated or *predominantly* fear-motivated. Those in both categories are daily becoming more and more aligned with their root motivational energy. They are tending increasingly to congregate with others of their own kind. This is why violence seems to be increasing in the post World War II era. It is. But so is love and well-being. Violence is increasing only among the fearful. Peace and good-will are increasing only among those who love. The growing violence is newsworthy and event-oriented, so the media is full of it. The growing love is subtle and process-oriented, and consequently seldom reported on the news.

Geographical locations are literally becoming either better or worse. Long before we are consciously aware of the separation process, we are subconsciously drawn where we need to be, to an environment that reflects our current cycle of purification. Upon becoming aware of this, few of us will find that we suddenly have to move. The chances are that if you are reading this book, you are already in an area where the energies of love are increasing.

Both love and fear draw people together regardless of religious, political, philosophical or racial allegiances, but they each have distinct forms of organizing the people on their respective wave lengths.

FEAR ORGANIZES PEOPLE MECHANISTICALLY, WHILE LOVE ORGANIZES PEOPLE ORGANICALLY.

For a while it is still possible to cross back and forth between these two increasingly polarized patterns of organization. But as the end of the appointed period draws near, the line begins to be drawn. It would not be true mercy to drag things out indefinitely. At some point the New Jerusalem descends out of heaven and the people who remain upon the earth commence a new epoch in conscious communion with God.

As I have traveled, it has been my observation that far more people are being drawn into love-rooted behavioral patterns than otherwise. My own feeling is that there will probably be only a few physical locations, almost certainly urban areas, where the fear energies will make their last stand. These will likely be destroyed in nuclear activity. Hopefully, such "die hard" situations will be rare. Like Lot's wife, we are cautioned not to look back.

Despite any appearances to the contrary, the earth is in good hands. All that is transpiring is contained within the single creative field of God's consciousness, occurring inside of God's own being.

Even the world of the 1980's and '90's, the world that some can see only in terms of international discord and economic instability, *even that world*, is contained within God's creative field. All things are unfolding to perfection. A millennia-old drama is playing itself out. Those who choose to perceive and energize the hate and the alienation will inhabit worlds where hate and alienation proliferate. Those who choose to trust in God share in a perspecitve of longer term.

THE VINE AND THE BRANCHES

Jesus spent His life on earth teaching people how to navigate through the separation process. A few were able to step into the synchronistic-time experience of this process 2,000 years ago, but until recently, human experience of the process has been rare. Now that we are living in the period when the separation is beginning to draw toward a conclusion, the teachings of Jesus are particularly pertinent.

> I am the true vine, and my Father is the husbandman. Every branch in me that beareth not fruit he taketh away: and every branch that beareth fruit, he purgeth it, that it may bring forth more fruit.
>
> John 15: 1-2

Jesus likens himself to a vine, to a single living system of which each man and women is a part. His Father, the universal botanical gardener, is keenly interested in this organism. He watches its branches closely. When one bears fruit, when it produces that which it was designed to produce, He prunes it, that it might produce more fruit. The branches of Christ's human family that do not bear fruit, perhaps whole cities, tribes and nations, are taken away.

Australopithecus, Homo erectus, Neanderthal and *Cro-Magnon* have all become extinct. They could not measure up to the qualities of spirit that the vine was designed to produce. There are many behavioral patterns and personality types common on earth today that are simply not sustainable in the changing spiritual climate brought about by Christ's coming.

In viticulture, the science of vine cultivation, pruning plays an important role. To prune means to remove something, to take something away that is superfluous or detrimental to the healthy development of the whole. Many of us who find ourselves consciously involved in the healing process discover that it is often as much a process of *unlearning* as it is of learning. It is a process of releasing fear-rooted concepts and behavioral patterns, *un*learning the false.

To those who begin to show promise of bearing fruit, to those who indicate an interest in awakening to a fuller life in Christ, the pruning shears of the Father are directed. We are led to recognize and eliminate behavior that is not in the Creator's (or our own) best interests. Reactive emotional habits, chronic anxiety, resentment, fear, self-righteousness, pride and a thousand and one other destructive tendencies are brought to our awareness that they may be eliminated. We are purged of that which saps our life force and diminishes the energy available for life-enhancing activities.

So it is collectively with every branch of the human family. Through the working of the law that governs the availability of His energies, the Father cultivates and prunes, taking away that which does not belong.

> I am the vine, ye are the branches. He that abideth in me and I in him, the same bringeth forth much fruit; for without me ye can do nothing . . . If a man abide not in me, he is cast forth as a branch, and is withered; and men gather them and cast them into the fire, and they are burned . . . If ye abide in me, and my words abide in you, ye shall ask what ye will, and it shall be done unto you.

> John 15: 5-7

In Christ's choice of the vine as a metaphor for the nature of His identity, He associates Himself with humanity in an intimate way. The vine is the network of Christ's love energies; the human family its dimensional branches; each healthy individual a manifestation of fruit. Through this parable, Jesus describes where divine energy exists, how it flows, how it is distributed and how human beings might live their lives within the range of its availability.

The words *"Abide in me and I in you"* point the way to an experience of the fullest physical, mental and emotional health. In the seventh verse of the fifteenth chapter of John Jesus elaborates: "If ye abide in me and my *words* abide in you, ye shall ask what ye will and it shall be done unto you."

When He speaks of His words abiding within, Jesus describes one of the characteristics of a unified state of God and man. To abide in one, God's words have to *live* within, they have to take up residence in one's heart. The kind of word Jesus is referring to here is not a linguistic statement, it is a *living word* that is actualized and shared. It is spoken aloud from the heart of each individual who is connected with the vine of Christ's entirety. It is a vibrant creative word, impossible to disassociate from action. It is the word that defines one in the nature of a specific role in the vine.

When such a word is abiding in an individual and that individual has accepted his or her true identity in Christ, " . . . ye shall ask what ye will and it shall be done unto you." When an individual knows him or herself as an aspect of Christ's living body on earth, the only request possible is that whatever is necessary for healthy growth be provided. Christ will never turn down such a request. How could He? The individual is in identification with the very life current of Christ. The Creator is vitally interested in his or her success!

In the 11th verse of the 15th chapter of John Jesus gives the reason for the parable of the vine and the branches. "These things I have spoken unto you *that my joy might remain in you, and that your joy might be full.*" Here is the nature of the life that flows through the vine. It is joyful! Joy accompanies the vital juice of the vine itself. Through Christ, it flows to every healthy individual.

Why has Christ's joy not been the emphasis of more theologians? Perhaps because joy would remain an elusive intangible for anyone who attempted to understand Christ without actually stepping into the current of his transformative nature. Only by full immersion in the living truth (which water baptism symbolizes) does one enter the life current of the vine.

Joy is a natural by-product of attunement to Christ's vine. When one puts the Kingdom of Heaven first, all necessary "things," including joy, are provided. As we move through our personal healing processes, we are not always able to experience joy at will. But we can always maintain the thankful attitude that opens the door to a fuller communion with Christ. He is never very far away.

"I am the wellspring of thy spirit," Christ might be saying, "bubbling up within you like a fountain that will never run dry. I am the source of your motivation; the vine as you are the branches. I have created you that you might share my joy, my life pulses through you. Let your trust in me be forever unwavering that my joy might abide in you and that your joy might be full."

ROADMAP OF THE KINGDOM

Thou shalt love the Lord thy God with all thy
heart and with all thy soul, and with all thy
mind. This is the first and great commandment. And the second is like unto it; thou shalt
love thy neighbor as thyself. On these two
commandments hang all the law and the
prophets.

Matthew 22: 37-40

The commandment "That ye love one another as I have
loved you," is for all people at all times, not just for those
privileged few disciples who were gathered around Jesus when
He first spoke these words. The sacred words AS I HAVE
LOVED YOU pertain to each one of us. We have each experienced Christ's love.

CHRIST'S LOVE IS NOT THE ABSTRACT ATTEN-
TIONS OF SOME DISTANT DEITY: IT IS EVERY
REAL LOVE YOU HAVE EVER KNOWN.

Christ's love is the love your mother and father shared at
your conception. It is the love your parents and relations gave
you as a child. It is the love you experienced with your first
adolescent romance. It is all the love that has ever guided and
protected you throughout your earthly life. All the love you
have ever known, whether you remember it or not, was
Christ's love flowing to you through one channel or another.
The wholeness of all the love you have ever given or received is
summed up in five little words: AS I HAVE LOVED YOU.

The commandment follows to love one another *with that much love*, with that quality and quantity of love. Why has this seemed so difficult?

In order to love others, we have first to be open to receiving love from God. Loving another as Christ loves us is a by-product of loving God with our all and receiving His love in return.

We are each aware of the precious love that we have received in our lives and the love that we are receiving even now. However, for most of us, this is but a fraction of the love that is available. The problem has been subconscious: most of us, to one degree or another, are afraid to receive Christ's love. A great deal of human energy is invested in avoiding the experience of love.

Why such a fear of love?

There is a strong pattern in our collective subconscious that is afraid to accept God's love because it senses the extent of change that the restoration of God's dominion on earth would imply. It knows that the values that have dominated the fallen state will be thoroughly shaken until there is not one stone of artificiality left standing upon another. It knows that a full acceptance of love would imply fundamental change.

This component of subconscious human irrationality is afraid of change, afraid of the unknown, afraid of healing. Yet the process of reasoning that led it to conclude that it had something to fear from God's love is based on an erroneous premise.

We can address this element of irrationality in ourselves and explain to it, as one would explain to a child, that its logic is faulty. We can assure it that receiving healing is in fact the most refreshing and enjoyable process imaginable. Healing is like a glass of water to the thirsty. Love is what lifts the burden of the weary and oppressed; it is not something to fear.

> Come unto me, all ye that labor and are heavy laden, and I will give you rest. Take my yoke upon you, and learn of me; for I am meek and lowly in heart: and ye shall find rest unto your souls. For my yoke is easy, and my burden is light.
>
> Matthew 11: 28-30

The behavioral options articulated by the truth of love are like directions telling an airplane how to fly, a dreaming man how to awaken, or a beacon how to shine. Refusing to receive them is as ridiculous as an automobile refusing to let anyone drive it or a lamp refusing to be plugged in. Without God's love we are but half creations, sleepwalking dreamers, incomplete angels. Yes, truth will introduce fundamental change, but this is what we have been designed for. This is our fulfillment, our greatest joy, our heart's delight. The kite has hung on the wall all winter. Spring has come. The children have taken the kite to the park to fly it. Is the kite afraid?

Subconsciously, the human family has feared that God might require more than they cared to deliver. Many of us are coming to see, however, that just the opposite is true. God requires precisely what we long to deliver. He requires our release from prison. He requires our polarity reversal. He requires the fulfillment of our deepest dreams. All God is asking from us is that we be ourselves, that we allow the reality of who we are in His sight to fully incarnate into our bodies, minds and hearts.

Jesus is offering us a road map. He is showing us the optimal route *through* the Last Judgment *into* the Kingdom of Heaven. He is helping us to relax during the removal of fear and fear-motivated behavior from our lives. Many people feel that Jesus' teachings are nice, but unattainable, ideals—good marks to shoot for, but impossible to embody in daily life. Nothing could be further from the truth.

JESUS' TEACHINGS ARE DESIGNED TO USHER US THROUGH THIS PERIOD OF PLANETARY BIRTH. THE ONLY REASON THEY MAY HAVE SEEMED DIFFICULT OR IMPOSSIBLE IN TIMES PAST IS BECAUSE PEOPLE HAVE ATTEMPTED TO APPLY THEM WITHOUT HAVING FULFILLED THE PREREQUISITE CONDITIONS THAT MAKE THEIR PRACTICE EASY AND NATURAL.

Jesus would not have laid the emphasis upon them that he did if his teachings were unattainable platitudes. Let us clear up any misconceptions about Christ's teachings being beyond our ability. Jesus would not have said, "Be ye therefore perfect, even as your Father in heaven is perfect," if the attainment of such a state were impossible. He would not have stated the first two commandments in such explicit terms if they were beyond human ability.

When your heart beats with the same creative pulsation that moves through your neighbors, when you are conscious of sharing the same purpose and essence, it is not difficult to love your neighbors as yourself. In a healthy state, it is not difficult to keep all the commandments. But one cannot arbitrarily *will* oneself into a healthy state. There is no short-cut to wholeness. There is a sequential healing process that takes place, a step-by-step procedure that removes the element of difficulty. The following chapter outlines this procedure and the qualities of spirit which overlight each of its seven steps.

VII

WHOLENESS

SEVEN STEPS TO WHOLENESS

THERE ARE A SERIES OF ATTITUDES THROUGH WHICH ONE MUST PASS IN ORDER TO ENTER THE STATE OF WHOLENESS THAT PREVAILS THROUGHOUT THE *BEING* OF GOD.

These are known as the attitudes of being, or the *Beattitudes*. The Beatitudes outline the process through which fear-rooted attitudes are transformed into radiant co-creative attitudes, attitudes in harmony with Christ's purposeful being. The first seven Beatitudes pertain to the healing process and might be looked upon as Seven Steps to Wholeness. Each step is characterized by one of the seven primary spirits before the throne of God.

The names that we will use to refer to these seven qualities of spirit need to be seen as only the best labels that the English language is able to provide. They are somewhat arbitrary. They are all aspects of love. The reality of the spirits overlap and flow into one another like the colors of a rainbow. Our labels unfortunately are not that fluid; but if we take these linguistic tags for the outer clothing of truth, and do not mistake them for the living reality of spirit, they can provide insight into what awaits those who embark on the Seven Steps.

1: PATIENCE

The first Beatitude is characterized by the *Spirit of Patience*. Patience is the first attitude that appears to guide the individual down the path of healing.

> Blessed are the poor in spirit: for theirs is the
> Kingdom of heaven.

> Matthew 5: 3

Blessed are the poor in spirit who are willing to face up to their fallen condition and to acknowledge their poverty of spirit. Blessed are those who upon finding themselves with a lack of vitality, do not fall into blaming their environment and the people around them, but who have the integrity to face up to their condition. Blessed are those who realize that the solution is not a material solution, but a spiritual solution, a matter of re-establishing contact with spirit.

The poor in spirit who recognize their poverty of spirit do not remain poor in spirit; "for theirs is the kingdom of heaven." They have planted the seeds for their return home. Still, those seeds have to germinate and grow in their own way and in their own time. The return to the Kingdom of Heaven does not necessarily have to take a long while, but is not often instantaneous. It would be foolish to say, "Well, I've recognized my poverty of spirit for a whole day now, where's the Kingdom of Heaven?" It is not advisable to dig up seeds to see if they are sprouting. The law works. Those who have acknowledged their poverty of spirit trust in the process that has been initiated. They let patience have her perfect way.

2: TRANQUILITY

> Blessed are they that mourn: for they shall
> be comforted.

> Matthew 5: 4

This Beatitude does not refer to those who weep and wail and bemoan their unfortunate lot. It pertains to those who truly mourn for the only thing worth mourning for: for the feel of the air stirring once again as God walks through the garden in the cool of the day, for communion with their Creator.

This Beatitude refers to those who mourn in longing for God's presence once again in the garden of their own bodies, minds and hearts. It speaks of those who mourn because they have come to recognize the barrier that they have placed between themselves and God. It speaks of those who are willing to step out from behind the bushes of concept and belief to greet God in the light, those who are willing to put down their barriers of shame and guilt to accept a new life in spirit.

Blessed are they who mourn for the only thing worth mourning for, for they shall be comforted. They will not mourn for long. This step is a short one, but the spirit that is born in this stage, the Spirit of Tranquility, continues on, as do the spirits born in each step. It sustains the soul throughout the healing process.

Once true mourning for paradise lost awakens in the human breast, God appears. He has been waiting for this attitude, this invitation, this welcome. He has been walking in the garden of each physical human body in the cool of every day since that body was born. In the fallen condition, the habit of hiding behind the trees of the garden has become so ingrained that most people remain unaware of God's presence within them. They have been hiding behind their images, their descriptions, their concepts of reality. They have been hiding behind a nervous network of images and illusions, afraid to pull the plug on their belief system and *see* God.

Mourning for paradise lost, mourning for the Edenic state where God and humanity live and breathe the same atmosphere of conscious cooperation, releases attention from the arbitrary structures that block perception. The Comforter comes. The Spirit of Tranquility washes the pathways and corridors of the body. The individual begins to develop the ability to stay focused on the healing process. Suddenly, it becomes real enough to the individual that he or she moves beyond *merely believing,* into the first stages of *actually experiencing.*

Things begin to return to proper perspective. Structures of doubt and anxiety no longer loom like great shadows devouring one's contentment. They appear for what they are: particles of dust in the eye of one immersed in the beauties of a New Heaven, passing clouds, nothing more. The first hints of the immensity of reality (as opposed to the trivia of fallen concerns) begins to dawn. Like the hunter who has finally caught sight of his quarry after long days of patient searching, the individual finds him or herself with a new ability to keep spiritual priorities in consciousness. Tranquility washes the soul. The long-awaited Comforter nurtures the spirit.

3: BLESSING

Blessed are the meek for they shall inherit the earth.

Matthew 5: 5

Based on observations that took into account only a small fraction of the fallen world during a short period of time, a man named Darwin once concluded that it was the fittest who survived. Unless fitness is seen in terms of wisdom and spiritual health, this is not accurate. It is not the fittest in the sense of physical strength and aggression who survive. It is not the violent with their offensive/defensive behavior who shall inherit the earth. It is the meek who now hold the key to survival.

The first earth that the meek inherit is the personal earth of the physical body. As the awakening man or woman inherits this earth, the body is blessed. This Beatitude is the third step toward redemption and healing. It is characterized by the *Spirit of Blessing*. This is the stage of the cycle when health returns, when the physical surroundings are blessed by renewed love. It is in this stage that inspiration occurs; new and creative ways of dealing with local circumstances are discovered.

The inheritance of the earth occurs slowly, giving the meek opportunity to develop their abilities of stewardship first over the personal, and then gradually, through the course of the remaining Beatitudinal steps, over the larger environment.

4: PURIFICATION

Blessed are they which do hunger and thirst after righteousness; for they shall be filled.

Matthew 5: 6

By this stage in the process, a good deal of inner healing has already taken place. The individual begins to hunger for some practical instruction in righteousness: in the right-use-ness of all things.

There is no way that anyone can truly hunger and thirst after righteousness without being filled, without receiving guidance and instruction. When one longs to make the inner experience of blessing an outer experience as well, reflected in all aspects of behavior, when one hungers and thirsts for the nonviolent paths of righteousness outlined by Jesus, instruction appears. The instruction can appear intuitively from within the individual, or it can appear outwardly through instruction from others who are willing to share their insights and experiences.

Collectively, the 1980's find humankind in the midst of this step. The true leaders of the human race are developing right livelihood.

This Beatitude, the Fourth Step to Wholeness, is characterized by the *Spirit of Purification.* Purification separates the fear frequencies from the love, the wheat from the chaff, self-centered behavioral patterns from creative avenues of stewardship. In this step assurance begins to put in an appearance. This is where things are brought out of the realm of theory and belief into the realm of practice. Distinctions become clear. It is no longer difficult to discern which behavior stems from God's love and which does not, which ideas, businesses and occupations are organized along positive channels of blessing and which are organized around greed. It is here that the individual begins to participate actively in the processes of separation in the external world.

5: JOY

Blessed are the merciful, for they shall obtain mercy.

Matthew 5: 7

Consciously participating in the separation process, beginning to share God's perceptions, allowing decisions to spring from love, one finds oneself at times acutely aware of the suffering that others are bringing upon themselves. But just because one is aware of the justice behind the causal/effect principle that guides all life, one does not disregard brothers and sisters who are suffering.

One who continues on in the great healing process that is outlined in the Beatitudes comes to develop the spirit of mercy. One *feels* God's forgiveness continuously available to those who are open to receiving it. One *experiences* the larger flow of God's life and *shares* in the radiance and differentiation of His spirit. One is naturally merciful. Receiving mercy oneself is automatic each time one has a failing or slip-up. In this fifth step, one begins to actively participate in God's healing of the larger human world. The *Spirit of Joy* characterizes those who have received mercy; it washes the last remaining distortion patterns from mind and heart.

6: WISDOM

> Blessed are the pure in heart, for they shall see God.
>
> Matthew 5: 8

The emotional realm becomes purified as the experience of being motivated by God's attitudes deepens. The heart is the interface between individual and God; it is where divine directives are first received and translated into attitude. Attitude precedes thought just as thought precedes action. Through a growing purity of heart one begins to see God, for one has begun to share in God's attitude, thought and action. As God's creative intentions are translated into action, one cannot help but notice earthly environmental factors beginning to clothe the previously invisible presence of God.

God's presence begins to act as an organizing principle upon the physical plane the moment a human heart becomes purified enough to accurately translate divine attitudes into actions. All events, substance, processes and relationships in the vicinity of the pure of heart begin to manifest the reality of God.

The pure of heart see the evidence of God, the manifest reality of God all around them. Soon, everything they see is God. Often the magnificence of their Creator and the processes of His manifestation on earth become so intriguing, so fascinating, so interesting, the pure of heart forget to pay attention to the things that are being separated out, the things that are falling apart and decaying. Soon it becomes natural to see God behind all that is transpiring.

This sixth step is characterized by the *Spirit of Wisdom*. This is where the seeds of wisdom come into maturity. The individual is becoming a literal part of God by this point, developing the capacities that help God continue His creative pursuits on earth. This sixth step is where one regains the ability to sense the timing of things, the season of things, no longer dissipating energy trying to do "good" at the wrong time in the wrong cycle. The pure of heart who see God share in God's perception. Integration characterizes all their undertakings.

7: UNCONDITIONAL LOVE

Blessed are the peace-makers, for they shall
be called the children of God.

Matthew 5: 9

Last we come to the peacemakers.

Many sincere men and women are working toward peace without awareness of the process that alone can bring it about. Peace is a laudable objective; but peacemaking skills do not come at the beginning of the healing process, they come at the end. The physician must first heal him or herself.

Those who attempt to implement a vision of peace without first developing inner peace are taking chances. It is possible they might do some good, but, like teen-agers borrowing a car without any training, they are just as likely to get into trouble. One can sincerely want to do some good and useful thing, like drive an automobile, but if one does not respect the mechanics involved, one will not have much success. There is a process that leads to peace; God is at the center of this process. A sincere desire for peace is not enough. War itself can spring from sincere but conflicting desires for peace.

In small congregations around the world, awakening sons and daughters of God are beginning to take steps toward sustainable peace. They are opening themselves to the attitudinal healing process outlined in the first seven Beatitudes. They are becoming the true harbingers of peace. They are at peace with themselves. They are at peace with God. They are not threatened by every passing breeze of violent thought. They feel a genuine compassion for the poor souls who are foolish enough to think anything can be gained through violence. A peacemaker who does not feel compassion for the violent is not a true peacemaker.

The two increasingly polarized groups of people on earth can be identified as follows:

* Those whose thoughts and behavior are violent, and

* Those whose thoughts and behavior are characterized by the attitudes of being.

For many, the term *nonviolence* has come to mean nothing more than simply avoiding violent means of problem solving. But this is looking at the problem from the problem's point of view. We know what creative attitudes are not; they are not violent. But what *are* they? This is the vital question that the peacemakers have answered. The children of God are having the experience of peace; it is the reality of their being. Their nonviolence is not abstinence; it is full to the brim with the peace of eternal being.

Just as the biosphere is but a thin film at the interface of earth and sun, so in the realms of spirit, every human action is but a surface film upon a vast ocean of being whose very nature is peace.

The peacemakers are called the children of God, because that is precisely what they are: the conscious offspring of the Creator Himself. The peacemakers are men and women who have adventured down the avenues of healing and caught the current of their divine identity. The children of God share the spirits and the purposes of God. The peacemakers have internalized the seven steps to wholeness outlined in the Beatitudes:

1) They recognize their faults.
2) They long for what they need to change.
3) They are gentle, unpretentious and nonviolent.
4) They pursue right livelihood.
5) They have compassion for others.
6) Their motivation is pure.
7) They offer unconditional love to all.

TOWARD A SUSTAINABLE PEACE

The peacemakers extend God's healing, comfort and blessing into a world in need of purification. Like Christ, they are teachers of forgiveness. They teach through example as well as through words. The peacemaker is willing to bring Christ into the marketplace, into business, into education, into the family kitchen, into all areas of living. In ways that are fitting, springing from a level of attunement where there is shared perception with Christ, the peacemaker spreads a lighthearted and friendly atmosphere.

As healthy children of God continue to multiply in the world, the laws of forgiveness and healing will come to be more thoroughly understood. People in need of healing themselves, their situations, or their nations will increasingly come to see that wherever disputes occur, the first step toward resolution is immediately to rule out the possibility of violence.

For many it is becoming a process of simple logic: the old way does not work; those who live by violence die by violence; therefore there must be a better way. Intelligent people are beginning to see that no one ever wins in an out-and-out battle. They know that this is true in their personal lives. They can see that it applies to all interaction.

VIOLENCE IS INEFFECTIVE, THE SHORTEST OF SHORT-TERM STRATEGIES.

Violence always creates more problems than it solves. It cannot do anything else. It is itself a child of fragmentation, a product of discord. No side is ever more right than another in a violent dispute. Both sides are partners in ignorance, spinning down a whirlpool of mutual annihilation.

The Creator has no interest in who was right or wrong yesterday. His interest is in healing the conflicts that trouble the human world. All are invited to allow the disputes of yesterday to fall away. This does not imply that things will remain as they are, or that the distribution of wealth, to give one example, will not change. The invitation is to accept the constant state of flux in which everything exists and trust that immutable laws regulate all God's worlds, even realms where injustice may momentarily seem to prevail.

People who are not willing to open themselves to the healing process are not the responsibility of the peacemaker. It does no good to force views upon those who are not open to receiving new insight. Where there is no openness to receiving healing, there is no real desire for peace. During the Last Judgment, there may be a few disputes in which the parties involved adamantly refuse to resolve their differences without violence. There is little that any of us can do about these. We can rest assured that the ensuing self-annihilation will be contained.

Every case of conflict is a case of the parties involved being out of touch with their own deeper motivations. Conflict is a child of reactive motivation; it springs from a failure to love. The last two Beatitudes caution us to not be deterred by conflicts that may arise while in the course of healing.

> Blessed are they which are persecuted for righteousness' sake: for their's is the kingdom of heaven.
> Blessed are ye, when men shall revile you and persecute you and shall say all manner of evil against you falsely, for my sake. Rejoice, and be exceeding glad: for great is your reward in heaven: for so persecuted they the prophets which were before you.
>
> Matthew 5: 10-12

There will likely be some contention during the weeks, months or years that may be required for the Beatitudinal healing process to recondition body, mind and heart. These last two Beatitudes caution us to not be deceived by appearances. They invite us to look to first things first, to ascertain that our own motives are correct, to do our best, to continue on in faith no matter what resistance, real or imagined, seems to appear in our paths.

We must never lose faith and think that some situation is too much for us. We are always capable of dealing with our situation creatively, as healers and peacemakers. If we fail at times, if we experience setbacks along the way, we do not hesitate, we do not get discouraged, we continue on. We are not blessed *because* we are persecuted, or *because* men say evil against us falsely, *but because we persevere* undaunted through these superficial illusions and remain true to the Spirit of God and His righteousness. Ours is then the Kingdom of Heaven.

We join all who have trodden upon this path, including Jesus Himself, in keeping first things first. Great is our reward in reality. We keep this passing historical interlude of healing in perspective. We hang in there. We care about what is real. We have full trust that God will settle all things fairly as the separation intensifies and draws toward the day of its conclusion; it is but a few passing moments in the spiritual adventure of eternity.

THE QUESTION OF GOD — AND EVIL

There is a species of oak in the Ozark Mountains that retains its dead leaves throughout the winter. Yet I do not remember ever having seen the dead leaves after the spring leaves have come out. During March and April, before the trees have opened their buds, I often walk through the forest hoping to catch the old leaves in the act of falling away. But I have never yet seen this take place. The old leaves do not actually fall away until the new leaves have come out. By then I am so filled with the springtime beauty of new life that I lose interest and forget to notice when the dead leaves finally let go.

We know that Christ's coming is bringing a thaw in the hardness of human hearts. We know that spring is on the move. It does little good to wonder what shall become of the dead leaves of the fallen world. They will fall away when they are supposed to. Our concern is with the new leaves coming into form all around us, with the appearance of Christ, in our hearts, in our personal worlds.

We can rest assured that the few dead leaves upon the vine of Christ's human family will not remain there forever. Even as you read, new leaves are unfolding in fresh life all around you. No doubt at some point a spring rain will come and wash the last leaves of yesteryear to the fertile forest floor. Lives rooted in violence and in fear will be removed. They are only a momentary part of our scenery. Their evil can only exist where there is a lack of intelligence.

Have you ever thought of it that way? Evil can only exist where there is a lack of intelligence.

It is difficult for me to take seriously those who propose that evil must accompany the appearance of that which is perfect, upright and beautiful. I have yet to see an example of a healthy organism where such is the case. This doctrine, that evil is necessary to creation, is an unholy stepchild of fallen human wisdom. Its rationale is deceitful.

There are true creative complementaries: light and dark, ocean and shore, time and eternity, male and female, inbreathing and outbreathing, energy and matter, spirit and form. Each of these creative complementaries form one pole of a single creative dyad. Each dyad sustains a healthy realm of interaction between its poles. But "evil" is no such critter; it is linked to no partner, creative or otherwise. It is the result of human ignorance and might more accurately be termed "disease." There is certainly no need or place for disease in a world restored.

The closest thing to "evil" in the natural order might be creative processes that in any given moment of time remain incomplete. This is divine "evol" in the sense of some *evol*utionary development yet unfinished, perhaps still looking a bit useless or incongruent to fallen human sensibilities. Divine "evol" is a far cry from *evil*, from humanly produced disease, suffering and illusion. We might do with a bit more humility in our philosophies.

Those awakening in spirit are often amazed at how little fallen humanity has actually seen. It makes good sense to withhold judgment until we are certain that we ourselves are functioning in health. There is no way we can understand the larger questions without first understanding ourselves as members of Christ's body. Fish swimming in the depths of the ocean, looking up and seeing the hulk of a great ship riding the waves above them might, on the basis of their perspective, propose all kinds of theories (entropy, evolution, thermodynamics, what have you). However, until they walked the decks of the ship in human form and shared the perspective of a gull looking down upon the ship from high above, their theories would be nonsense; they would remain half-truths, fragments of wholeness, hollow speculations and nothing more.

God is inviting us to share His way of looking at things. He is calling us up out of the darkness of our historical ignorance. We are invited to inhabit the realms of consciousness where answers abound, where truth lives in us, around us, through us, permeating all that we are. It is refreshing to let these smug human theories fall like shackles from our souls, to stand up, to give our hearts, our minds, our attention to our Creator's voice.

Do you hear it?

Do you hear God's voice echoing throughout the garden in the cool of today?

"Where art thou?" He asks.

Perhaps we are the answers to God's prayers. He has certainly asked a question.

LEARNING TO STAY INSPIRED

In a modern recording studio, there are at least 32 separate "tracks" upon which the various components of a musical composition may be recorded. The studio technicians recording a vocal piece will dub (or superimpose) track upon track of instrumental recordings, one upon the other, until the instrumental aspect of the song is complete. Then the vocal, or vocals, are added.

Inspirational levels of thought proceed from their source in God like steady ever-changing instrumental sound tracks upon which the individual is invited to function. There are billions of inspirational levels of thought, each one complete unto itself, each one proceeding from a point of light within the mind of God and compatible with all the others. There is in fact *one* specific inspirational frequency for each human being. The inspirational levels of thought radiating throughout the eternity of God's being fall into seven general categories, each one correlating with one of the Seven Spirits of God, one of the seven colors of the rainbow, one of the seven notes in the Western musical octave. All the levels of inspiration are interwoven; essences of each penetrate all others. God dubs them together in universal symphony. Each one lives a melody.

An individual melody line has a tremendous range of variation available to it. Any jazz player knows there are numerous harmonies, octaves, and thousands of improvisational options that can complement a basic background rhythm of chords and bass notes. In much the same way, each individual has an almost infinite range of choice regarding the style of a lifetime in sync with the specific inspirational level designed for him or her. Even within the individual's primal inspirational level, there are multiple sub-levels pertaining to all creative areas of interest.

Humanity as a whole is designed to function upon more general inspirational frequencies of thought, furthering the interests of both themselves and creation. These inspirational frequencies are not a prison. Free will has tremendous scope within the range of their energy. However, *these inspirational levels of thought are the only place where the energy flows.* To move outside the range of their expression is to depend upon an intermediary energy source, a middle-man, that steals the inspirational energy and then sells a small portion of it back at the stiff price of suffering, misery and premature death. To step outside of the range of one's designated level of inspiration is like moving from a lush and fertile climate to the edge of the arctic. One can do so if inclined, but it hardly seems wise.

The experience one has while thinking in a healthy manner on his or her designated level of inspirational thought can not be compared to conventional fallen thinking. The emotional realm is thoroughly involved. The spiritual interest is entirely present. One rides a tangible current of energy and improvises within the energy-parameters available. Each thought track is one of the *intentions* of the Creator. There are levels of inspiration that pertain to architecture, engineering, physics, sociology, literature, agriculture, biology—any creative field of human endeavor that one might care to explore.

We have all had some experience with inspirational levels of thought. Most of us, even in the fallen state, cannot help but stumble upon them from time to time. These are the times when we are making love, when we are having new creative ideas, when we are occupied with music, poetry, art, or if we are lucky, our occupation. Thinking is not difficult at these times; ideas and images flow easily and naturally.

The coming of Christ to collective human consciousness can be understood in terms of these multiple levels of inspirational thought.

When I first began to understand *how* Christ was coming and how far His advent into human consciousness had already progressed, I was amazed that I had not seen the obvious sooner. *Christ has already come on all the finer levels of human thought.*

The Creator's plan to keep the Fall from becoming fatal was to begin slowly penetrating areas of human creativity until more and more human beings were contacting His Seven Primary Spirits on these Channels. This ingenious approach holds the moment of actual human polarity reversal in the steady hands of maximum continuity. It provides a maximum degree of consistency during the Last Judgment for those individuals with experience upon inspirational channels.

Christ is now present in much of the human heaven. This is why the past 2,000 years have been so remarkable in terms of technological progress. During the two millennia since Christ's Ascension it has become progressively easier for human thinkers and inventors to spend time on these creative channels of inspiration. Many have brought their insights back with them to the fallen world. Unfortunately, the implementation and utilization of what was gleaned from these levels has remained tainted by survival fears. Consequently, the human *attitudes* that have implemented these insights have remained unchanged.

WE FIND OURSELVES IN AN AGE WHEN OUR TECHNOLOGY IS REFLECTING AN INTELLIGENCE WE HAVE YET TO APPLY IN OUR RELATIONSHIPS.

Christ took some risk in placing all this technology in the hands of emotional children. Yet He has the means at His disposal to trigger polarity reversal at any moment. He only postpones the moment of awakening so that a greater number might be included among the saved.

Many of us have traveled in and out of inspirational thought without having realized what we were doing, without having ever become conscious of the process, without having ever tried to use our intelligence to stay on those inspirational frequencies.

It is useful to recognize the *not-doing* that the subjective identity experiences *prior to engaging* with Christ's inspiration. There is a short interval, not unlike putting in a clutch when shifting gears on a vehicle, an interval of not-doing that precedes the transition to inspirational thought.

Jesus called it *prayer.*

In the fallen state, people are programmed to DOING. Even when bodies have stopped, minds randomly churn out ideas and associations. These take place in the first heaven where fallen sensibilities dwell. The first heaven has historically been the origin of human behavior. Even many who long to know Christ continue the almost incessant DOING of self-reflective thought.

Not-doing allows Christ's consciousness to flow out from within you like a mighty spring that will never run dry. As you experience Christ's perception flowing out through you, you enjoy *watching* how His awareness translates automatically (like water taking the path of least resistance) into the optimal next move for you. Whatever subject area Christ's consciousness encounters, it translates automatically, instantly, into the optimal pattern of interaction *for you* in that situation. This is what it means to share Christ's VISION.

Nothing is predestined except the location and availability of conscious energy on your personal frequency of inspiration. You proceed with your own stylized behavioral improvisation. You carry Christ's VISION as your energy-resource guidebook. You see what Christ's purposes are in your vicinity. You see the way He has designed your physical circuitry, like a race car tailored to a particular track through the dimensional worlds.

Through prayer, you immerse yourself in God's will as it is done on inspirational levels in heaven. As this translates into action, God's creativity manifests through you on earth.

The not-doing that opens the door to this is more than just the absence of inner and outer activity; it is a rich experience of BEING, bringing the realization of oneself as one of Christ's terrestrial representatives. When you are neither troubled nor afraid, when you are still inside, when your heart is easy and relaxed, you share a Creator's experience.

It really is simple.

Put in the clutch through prayer. Shift the consciousness into awareness of inspirational thought. Release the clutch and spiral into a new state of conscious function in communion with God.

VOLUNTEERING FOR NEW JERUSALEM

A mantra or the repetition of the rosary can help to rhythmically align Creator and created on subconscious levels, but this does not offer the full conscious communion that is the nature of true prayer. Conscious communion with God does not require repetition.

> But when ye pray, use not vain repetitions as
> the heathen do, for they think that they shall
> be heard for their much speaking.

Matthew 6: 7

Jesus offered instruction regarding the nature of prayer. He outlined *the attitudes* that constitute effective prayer. Words may articulate an attitude, they may lead to an attitude, but it is the attitude that provides the energy that communicates prayer.

ATTITUDES ARE THE ENVELOPES IN WHICH WE SEND OUR THOUGHTS TO GOD.

Attitudes also provide the return envelopes in which we receive God's reply. The specifics we have to share with God are like the letter that goes in the envelope. When we pray as Jesus taught us, we convey to Him the essences of our immediate situation. We deliver specifics, but do not request specifics. We show Him ourselves and our world. We open ourselves to His inspection and love.

> Your Father knoweth what things ye have
> need of before ye ask him. After *this* manner

therefore pray ye: Our Father which art in heaven, Hallowed be thy name. Thy kingdom come. Thy will be done in earth, as it is in heaven. Give us this day our daily bread. And forgive us our debts, as we forgive our debtors. And lead us not into temptation, but deliver us from evil: For thine is the kingdom, and the power, and the glory, for ever. Amen.

Matthew 6: 8-13

In oneness with our mother the earth, in oneness with the earth of our physical bodies, in oneness with our possessions, in oneness with all that we perceive, we turn to face Our Father in Heaven, the Spirit that calls us into being. Our Father, our point of spiritual origin, our source, lies in heaven. Our spiritual roots extend into a nonphysical realm where we have our conscious source. We turn, in oneness with the earth, to greet Our Father.

We respect, honor and celebrate your nature of wholeness, O Father. *Hallowed,* Anglo Saxon root, *hal,* meaning whole, "be thy name." *Name,* signifying nature. Our Father's nature is whole. "Our Father, our spiritual source beyond this earth, your nature is wholeness."

"Thy kingdom come, thy will be done in earth, as it is in heaven."

We are in touch with our source. Our attitude indicates the respect for God's nature that will enable us to monitor His frequency. We acknowledge our Father's purposes and open ourselves to the entrance of these purposes into our lives. We indicate our willingness to allow the extraterrestrial purposes of Universal Spirit to be done in the sphere of earth for which we are responsible *as they are done in heaven.* We are open to allowing our relationships with all things to be restructured on a new basis, in a new way, with new premises and new implications.

It is hard to imagine how anyone could be aware of God's incredibly wonderful purposes without wishing to pursue them. I can not imagine anyone who would not feel at least some curiosity, if not an outright sense of adventure. When we pray, "thy will be done in earth as it is in heaven," we are volunteering our part of the world as a beachhead for the grounding of Christ's conscious coming! We are opening our hearts to receive the intentions of the Creator into our lives, so that what He has designed as our creative range of function, will in fact be the range in which we live. We are volunteering for the New Jerusalem! But we have to really mean it.

Our words communicate to God on the surface. Our attitudes communicate to Him underneath. If our words are to be intelligible to God, they have to correlate with our attitude.

The Lord's Prayer is an attitudinal journey.

As we pray more frequently and more effectively, new attitudes come to characterize our lives. We find ourselves more open to spontaneity, to risk-taking, to change. Not for their own sakes, but because we learn that it is often down these pathways that Our Father seeks to lead us.

There may be some for whom the words, "thy kingdom come, thy will be done, in earth as it is in heaven," do not imply change. But I suspect these are few. For most of us these words are a call to adventure. It would not be accurate to portray them in any other light.

ADVENTURE IN THE
ARCHITECTURE OF LIGHT

On this adventure there is a rule.

To enjoy the material realms and to avoid becoming mesmerized by them, we have to take ourselves lightly.

Part of the pleasure of incarnation relates to the serious way in which matter takes our purposes. The earth's inherent seriousness is well-intentioned, but it can be devastating when allowed to get out of balance. We are to release all slights, debts, injustices, trespasses *as they occur.* We are not to incur debts that hold our attention in the past. When we incur debt, we miss what is occurring in the present. We take ourselves out of the range for which we were designed. We fail to notice what is right in front of our eyes.

Suppose our journey is through a jungle. The fruit is hanging off the trees all around us. Much of it we have never tried before. We are in this moment of the dimensional jungle for the first time, so we may not initially recognize the fruit as edible. When our attention is in the present, we notice things, we see God's provision. His insight runs through us like the bass notes in our song. We are provided for.

"Give us this day our daily bread. And forgive us our debts as we forgive our debtors."

The two sentences are linked.

Jesus is stating a law. This is how universal abundance operates. When we forgive our debtors, *we* are forgiven. Under no circumstances do we receive God's forgiveness when we still hold some slight from the past. When a spirit of petty complaint or silent resentment is present, forgiveness cannot take place, for the past has not been released; we are not open to receiving. Daily bread is not provided.

When we think about the times when our lives worked and compare them to the times when they did not, we often notice that when things were not going well, we were resentful or angry. When things were going well, we had forgotten such pettiness.

The provision of daily bread is with us moment by moment. It stands to reason that there is abundance in the presence of God. To share in that abundance, we have to enter God's presence, and we have to fulfill the requirements of whatever it takes to stay in that presence. The present moment is where we perceive the wheres and hows of abundance.

For those in right function, it becomes second nature to forgive, forget and move on. But the challenges do not end there. For me it has been like peeling off layers of an onion skin. There always seems to be another layer beneath the last one, each layer a little more intimate, each opening my awareness to an ever higher state of consciousness, each new insight making me feel like something of a blind man for not having seen it sooner. Each successive realization that I have come to (usually pertaining to some previously unconscious behavioral pattern) has been simpler than the last. With every layer that falls away, I find that I am more aware of the incredible extent to which God has gone to keep us in His favor, in His light, in the range of His energy and awareness. In fact, He has made it rather difficult to fall out of His favor. We have only to pray and we are surrounded with assistance.

"And lead us not into temptation, but deliver us from evil." Help us, Father, to remain unswayed by the crafty posturing of fear. Deliver us from the chaos that is born of fear's logic. Help us to remember that upon which hinges the law and all the prophets; love for you, love for our neighbor, and action motivated by love.

We have traveled the corridors of God's love. Perceiving them again, we come home. Those who have said it is difficult to keep Christ's teachings could not have seen His purposes sketched in the heavens, revealed in the organic architecture of light—an organism of potentiality spiraling from eternity into eternity. Those who have glimpsed this wonder find it difficult to do anything *but* keep Christ's commandments.

It is hard work using our free will to counter all our better inclinations. Continuously bucking the natural flow is much more difficult than healthy function. Still, the neon signs of our habits beckon us down their familiar alleyways, We pray, "deliver us from evil." Spare us the nonsense. We want to come home to your awareness, O Universal Spirit. We mean what we are saying. Our attitude coincides with our words. This is not vain repetition. We feel the atmosphere quiver with every word, "For thine is the kingdom and the power and the glory, for ever. Amen."

Many feel that it is blasphemous to put something as sacred as the Lord's Prayer into your own words.

I disagree.

It seems to me that Jesus spent the better part of His ministry teaching us that the central activity of our lives should be precisely that: translating the Lord's Prayer into our own living experience—our own words.

THE LORD'S PRAYER

OUR FATHER, THE ESSENCE OF OUR MOTIVATION, OUR POINT OF ORIGIN BEYOND TIME AND SPACE, WE GREET THEE. THY NATURE IS WHOLENESS. MAY THY CONSCIOUSNESS COME AND MAY THY CREATIVE INTENTIONS PREVAIL, IN THE FLESH OF OUR BODIES AND IN THE SPHERE OF OUR MOTHER EARTH, AS THOSE SAME CREATIVE INTENTIONS ALREADY PREVAIL IN THE REALMS OF SPIRIT BEYOND. GIVE US THIS DAY OUR DAILY BREAD, A SYMBOL OF THE SPIRITUAL NOURISHMENT WE REQUIRE. WE KNOW THAT ALL OUR NEEDS WILL BE PROVIDED AS WE REMAIN CONNECTED TO THEE AS A PART OF THY WHOLENESS. WE REMAIN HEALTHY BY LETTING YOUR LOVE FLOW THROUGH US,

RELEASING THE DEAD LEAVES OF YESTER-
DAY'S EXPERIENCE, FORGIVING ALL REAL
AND IMAGINED INJUSTICES. IN THIS WAY WE
ARE OPEN TO THE FORGIVENESS THAT IS
ALWAYS AVAILABLE FROM YOU. LEAD US
ALONG THE CURRENTS OF THY LOVE AND
DELIVER US FROM THE TENDENCIES TOWARD
JUDGMENT THAT RESTRICT OUR AWARENESS
OF THEE. LET US LIVE EACH MOMENT IN
COMMUNION WITH THY SPIRIT, A BRANCH
ON THE VINE OF THY TERRESTRIAL BODY,
ALWAYS HONORING THE SOURCE OF OUR LIFE
IN THEE: FOR THINE IS THE KINGDOM AND
THE POWER AND THE GLORY, FOREVER. AMEN.

WAGES IN THE KINGDOM

It is beautiful how simply the Lord's Prayer works. Once we stop blaming others for our experience, we stop blaming ourselves as well. Suddenly we feel good about ourselves, better than we have felt about ourselves for years. We begin to receive God's grace, God's favor. We notice ways of extending service that will support us in the process.

The way people are nourished in the Kingdom is not unlike the earth: each one provides a service and, as a matter of course, is provided for along the way. But in the first heaven and the first earth, people have had it backwards; they provide services *because* they are trying *to get* supported. In the new heaven and the new earth, people's lives are 100% recreation and service. Their salary, their means of support, is a secondary *effect* produced by their service.

When there is a willingness to let God's will be done on earth and a willingness to let go of the blame nonsense that causes a reduction in the flow of God's love, daily bread is assured. In the flowing current of God's love, bread has its origin, This is where Christ's body and blood are found. The earth bread that we bake is just a shadow, a pale imitation, of the living nourishment of the Spirit of truth.

The Spirit of truth dances along the circuitry of God's love. He is the architect, the builder, and the foreman of the construction crew that will allow God's plans to come into form. He is looking for men and women to help him in this work. He pays an excellent wage. He pays us what he knows will enable us to live well. But to receive the wages of truth, we have to be able to receive God's love.

On the surface there would seem to be little correlation between poverty and an inability to forgive, but the two are intimately associated. When we do not forgive ourselves or others, we limit our ability to receive love. Fundamentally, material necessities are forms of love. They are part of the provision that is designed to flow through our lives on the currents of love. Unless we forgive, we cannot receive.

A lack of forgiveness always indicates a lack of trust. To whatever degree we do not trust, God does not trust us with His life-giving energy. Our own lack of trust is telling Him that we are not responsible. We are like traffic directors directing the current of God's sustenance. When we do not trust God or ourselves in certain areas, corresponding body parts receive a reduction in current. The same blockages that produce disease in the physical body clog up the channels of abundance that are designed to provide our material needs.

Everything that we require is provided as we immerse ourselves in love, including financial and material necessities.

When Jesus said, "Seek ye first the Kingdom of Heaven and all things will be added unto you," he was articulating this law. When Christ's love initially touches a fallen man or woman, its first translation, the first form it takes, is forgiveness; its second translation is healing; its third is pure, unqualified love, *bringing with it all material needs.*

Each creature is designed to receive energy and sustenance in a specific way, using what is received to implement the purpose for which it was created. Our sustenance flows to us through designated channels that we block when we hold on to a sense of injustice. In the healthy state we are nourished as any organic system, as the earth nourishes us now in fact, but without fear-rooted intermediaries. The Lord's Prayer outlines the laws that govern the receipt of all that is signified by "daily bread." Each of us has the opportunity to step into the currents of God's grace and discover these laws of nourishment for ourselves.

We have traced all forms of terrestrial energy back to the sun, but we often forget that the sun itself is our most ancient symbol for love.   Ultimately, all nourishment, physical, psychological, emotional and spiritual, springs from a common source in God's eternal love. To the degree that one is able to abide in love, necessities are provided. The love that God feels for the earth and her creatures is shared by those who awaken Christ's nature within them; Christ's love and their own love become inseparable.

One cannot passionately love the earth and her creatures and long to see terrestrial life-forms returned to a state of health and not prosper. The earth and her provision responds to such love as surely as to the light of the summer sun. Wherever it is in expression, love will heal, love will bring clarity. And love will provide.

PERFECTION

There are no "levels" of spiritual development. Among those who have moved through the Beatitudinal healing process, there are only equals. In the fallen state, one may be healthier than another, but among those who have received healing, there is no hierarchy.

In the execution of specific practical projects, like the construction of a building, the making of a movie or the healing of a planet, there will naturally be a range of skill and division of responsibility. This will find certain individuals with authority in certain areas, but all are essential to the whole and all are *spiritually* equal.

In the healthy state, each individual has a specific field of responsibility, *and full authority in that area.* Working together with others similarly designed, individuals are fulfilled and the purposes of the whole are served. This is the meaning—and the only meaning—of perfection.

> Be ye therefore perfect, even as your Father
> which is in Heaven is perfect.
>
> Matthew 5: 48

The kind of perfection that is experienced by conscious sons and daughters of God is not the end result of a long process. It is accepting oneself and all things in their present stage of development. Perfection is not static, it is flowing, fluid, growing, changing, alive. The universe itself is an interwoven matrix of living processes, clothing spirit in ever-changing form. There is no frozen, ultimate perfection. Eternally all things continue to grow, always revealing new potential. Perfection is accepting one's situation *as it is* and then consciously assisting in the release of its inherent potential.

One who is perfect does not make a great issue of either success or failure, both of which still occur. Such an individual looks at all things and moves on, accepting himself or herself *as is* in each moment. Consequently, he or she is perfect, not because there is no more potential to reveal—for that will never happen—but because he or she appreciates the unfolding perfection of all that is.

Perfection is being immersed in the process of healthy unfoldment. It has nothing to do with the *quantity* of the potential that is brought forth. When we accept Christ into our daily lives, we enter the process and immediately begin to experience perfection. Christ draws forth inner talents, hidden capabilities, unsuspected gifts. The actualization of each fresh potentiality raises the stakes of one's opportunities and calls for a yet further manifestation of inherent design.

As it comes into form on earth, each one's potential reveals God's design for him or her. It is not a closed system. An individual's capacity for revelation is as great as God's, for God is the source of all potential.

The possibilities for creative expression inherent within radiation-range of this local star and mother planet are limitless. Though certain stages, fulfilling certain objectives, will be met, potential will never be exhausted. The nature of creativity is to use every new objectification of potential as a springboard into a whole new level of unfoldment. Potential feeds upon its own release. We see hints of the infinite capacity for creation when we examine the subatomic world or turn our attention to the billions of galaxies that surround our own. How many worlds? How many experiences? How many wonders?

Perfection is being thankful for the privilege of participating in the process.

HONING OUR UNIVERSAL GAME SKILLS

B. J. Palmer, a great healer of recent times and founder of Chiropractic Medicine, used to have a sign over his office door that summed up an attitude he found particularly conducive to good health: "Don't take life so damn seriously," it advised.

It helps to keep a sense of humor. We have mistakes yet to see. They have their sorrowful sides at times. But as the healing process brings recognition of our mistakes, our situations are not without their lighter sides. We should never fear looking at our mistakes. They are little things, dust in the eye, no big deal once we see them. It is only as we do not see them that problems continue.

The best way to eradicate counterproductive behavior from our lives may be to start off by not regarding our shortcomings quite so fatalistically. Why not think of the challenges we encounter in our healing process as a game?

Imagine a computer with a game program set at precisely the level of difficulty that would allow you to win by a narrow margin while simultaneously exercising the skills you most need in order to better understand the game. Our immediate situation is *always* like that. The world around us is continuously offering to us Precisely-What-We-Need 101. Life will always be challenging. We might as well learn to enjoy the challenges.

In pool, chess, or tennis we often refer to our partner as "our opponent." A good opponent is matched to the skills of his or her partner and will always help his or her partner develop greater skill. When Jesus says in the 36th verse of the 10th chapter of Matthew, "And a man's *foes* shall be those of his own household," he is not alluding to anyone who is out to get us. That is the trouble with translations sometimes; if we read only with our heads and do not involve our hearts, we may misunderstand. Thankfully, no one is out to get anyone. Our *foes* are the friends with whom we enjoy a good game of life once in a while.

In the course of living with others—siblings, parents, spouses, children, friends, neighbors, co-workers, whoever—class is in session. This is not the time to preach our theories and complain because others do not subscribe to them. This is the time to live what we know the truth to be, to put into practice, into action, the implications of all that Jesus taught and demonstrated. The others of our own household are our *worthy opponents,* matched to our skills.

We find that our worthy opponents are ever challenging us to be more real, more honest, more patient, more straightforward, more forgiving, more lighthearted, more loving: in other words, more ourselves. The *foes* of our own household are our truest friends as we are theirs. They are in the best position of all our acquaintances to help us grow in the ways of spirit. If we look at our interaction as a game, we find it is a game we all win. Each moment provides what we need to "stretch the envelope" of our limitations just a bit more.

Once the sound barrier was commonly believed to be impregnable. The early pilots thought of it as a sort of brick wall in the sky. There turned out to be no such thing. Neither is there any ceiling on our potential. There is only a decisive turning point after which nothing will ever again be the same. Our craft may seem to be taxed to the limit as we approach this point. We may feel some butterflies, a bit shaky, but God's word is to continue on, to go for it, to break through the world pattern. Jesus demonstrated time and again how one moves through that barrier. It can be done. The barrier is no more than a collective illusion. Beyond it is a new world, shimmering in the morning light, beckoning to our souls.

We do not honor popular illusions. We do not refuse to sail to the new world because others hold that the earth comes to an abrupt end in a great abyss where demons dwell. What nonsense! We have seen her shadow on the moon; we know our world is whole. We know our bodies, minds and hearts are up to the challenge of Christ's perfection. We know we are designed to break through even the subtlest of fallen human habits. We have the spirit, the insight, the perseverance, the determination to crack the code, to see how we have been programmed by our fears. And to change.

Our historical programming is invalid. Its continuation will destroy our physical creations. We see beyond it, remain undaunted and move on, determined, in love, no longer willing to remain separate from our beloved. If we are capable of being intimidated by our fears, we will have to face them before the victory. But so what? We have come here to heal, to transform and to assist Christ in the birthing of a universal species. Where is our sense of adventure? This is the ultimate game, the challenge of life in our times.

VIII

RESURRECTION

THE CRUCIFIXION/RESURRECTION CONTINUUM

THE CROSS is the symbol for all who follow Christ. It depicts the convergence of all creative dyads. It represents the single point where all complementary creative partners, such as matter and energy, male and female, time and space, love and truth, come together in dynamic union. The cross represents the meeting ground of Creator and creation. It symbolizes the surface of the earth interfacing with the sun through biological activity. In the most immediate and human sense, the cross is where Christ meets your particular environment.

> If any man will come after me, let him deny himself, take up his cross daily, and follow me.
>
> Luke 9: 23

If anyone shall follow Christ in His creative purposes, if any shall follow the energy that is available within the range of His creative intentions, he must deny what he has thought himself to be, pick up a new identity in Christ's nature and follow the currents of Christ's love. Just as the acorn must stop thinking of itself in the unbroken terms of a seed, specific and clear-cut, and open itself to the death of bursting asunder in revelation of inner potential, so the individual who would follow Christ must die to all past self-identities. He or she must release all the old assumptions, addictions and demands, the good as well as the ill, and take up the cross of relationship in the presence and nature of Christ.

In the personal sense, the cross symbolizes everything with

which we are involved: our habits, thoughts, friends, hopes and fears. If we would follow Christ, we must lift up the cross of our time/space situation and allow ourselves and all things around us to become suspended in on-going creative action. We must lay down our fictitious lives as isolated individuals to discover our true lives in spirit.

If it appears that there is a sacrifice involved, it is only apparent. Carrying one's cross, moving with one's life purpose, truly being oneself is a joyous experience. The notion that it is some great ordeal is incorrect. Jesus could hardly have stated it more plainly, "The yoke is easy and the burden is light." Carrying one's cross *is* fulfillment. It is what life is all about.

When you get right down to it, we do not have much choice as to whether or not we are going to take up the cross of our time/space situation. When we chose to incarnate, we chose to do precisely that. Our only choice at this late date is as to *how* we take up our cross. Will we take it up in the victorious nature of Christ? Or will we take it up as miserable little unfortunates, at the mercy of every passing environmental whim? In the first instance we are lifted up with Christ into the service of universal intelligence. In the second, we are crucified.

Jesus moved *through* the experience of the crucifixion *into* the experience of resurrection. He showed the way for each individual to do the same. We are invited to willingly accept our own crucifixion in the fallen state and then to continue on undaunted into the experience of our own resurrection, never stopping or admitting defeat until we join once again with our Creator in consciousness.

THE CROSS NEEDS TO BE SEEN AS A LIVING PROCESS, FLOWING FROM ILLUSION INTO REALITY, FROM APPARENT DEATH INTO LIFE ETERNAL.

The cross is a powerful symbol for Christ, indeed for all the Christian world, not because of the crucifixion in and of itself, but because of the resurrection that drew the crucifixion (and all that it represented) up into life eternal. If we are to leave the impotent Christianity of dogma and step into the transformative Christianity of the living Christ, we need to understand the crucifixion as a process flowing into the resurrection.

We cannot isolate the crucifixion as a snapshot of reality focusing on Christ's death apart from the resurrection and understand the significance of the cross. The significance of the crucifixion is not *death on the cross* but *life on the cross.* " . . . I am come that they might have life, and that they might have it more abundantly." (John 10: 10) It is Christ's life that we are invited to share at the intersecting cross of our particular juncture of time and space. It is not a death, which did not prove sustainable, that is to occupy our primary attention. It is a living experience.

Christ's greatest offering to the human race, indeed to all time and history, is His life. He, Himself, *is* the Way, the Truth and the Life. The true cross is not a symbol of death. It is a living symbol of our awakening from the death-like slumber of historical ignorance into the conscious presence of God.

The New Christian Experience is symbolized by a cross that is centered in the reality of a living Christ. It is rooted in the dynamic, living, breathing creative cross of Christ's temporal relationship. The burden of the true cross is light. The true Christian picks up his or her situational cross and begins living in a world of light, following Christ in the expression of love, assisting Christ in the awakening of a human family.

The cross that we bear is the cross of union, representing the intersection of a Creator's unity and a creation's diversity. We stand with Christ at the balance point between time and eternity, between light and substance. We represent the truth of Christ in a specific field of creative interaction. We share Christ's light. We are facets of a single universal intelligence, lights unto the world.

THE PROMISE OF RENEWAL

In the beginning we walked with the Lord God in the cool of the day. We walked with eternal creative spirit as one. There was no separation of consciousness. In the patterns of potentiality that danced up around God and followed Him like a rainbow aura, we saw human possibilities. We knew the risks. We were cautioned. We dove in. It was a bit like trying to get into a space suit, a bit awkward, but when it was done there was a whole new realm of creative mobility available.

> Let *us* create man after *our* image, after *our* likeness.
>
> Genesis 1: 26

In partnership with Him who was and is before all worlds, as conscious aspects of God, we blessed human beings with our life. Through the power of our love we drew their bodies into being. Then, as we know, a malfunction occurred. There was a failure in the system. The minds that the human creatures were developing became self-active, caught up in their own feedback, closed in upon themselves. They were no longer open to the direct influence of our love, no longer responsive to the guidance of our truth. *Their* development and *our* incarnation were halted. The process was far from complete, the creation unfinished. The humans had rebelled in a leaderless, senseless revolt. It soon began to degenerate into chaos. We needed to communicate with them.

Two thousand years ago, we succeeded in establishing a point of contact. Through Jesus of Nazareth, Christ was able to incarnate, the essence, representative and leader of us all. The ice was broken. Jesus began to heal and to teach. He knew that this was not the time for the collective resurfacing of His/our spirit through the human beings on earth, but He planned to do what He could, sowing as many seeds as possible.

Seeds.

The seeds of the vegetable kingdom are very wise. They do not open and begin to develop until the conditions for their growth and proliferation are optimal. There is a species of pine cone in the American Northwest that will lay dormant for hundreds of years if need be, designed to withhold its fertile life until a fire in the forest has eliminated all competition. If the seeds of the plant world are this wise, how much wiser the seeds of transformation, planted by Our Lord!

It was necessary that a few seeds release the fullness of their potential there in the dark beginnings of Western culture in order to ensure that our traditions would be sufficiently imbued with truth. This resulted in the flowering of the early Christian Church. However, since the Third Century, A. D., Jesus' teachings have for the most part remained neglected and untried. They have lain dormant while Christ prepared the heaven, waiting for the day when they would sprout from within human tradition to meet Christ at the dawn of a new era.

Christ knew well that the greatest obstacle to His return would be the same that had met Him in Israel, the entrenched traditions of the fearful. To plant, at the very core of these traditions, the vital seeds of a dynamic truth would greatly undermine the ability of tradition to deceive the elect; it would maximize the number of the saved.

Christian tradition is like a grounding rod, driven deep into the core of Western sensibilities, gradually being electrified by current events. It was implanted 2,000 years ago by a man, interacting with the cultures of His day, while still directed by the will of His Father in Heaven.

Through Jesus, all of us had a point of representation, a point of radiation, into the earth. Many human beings found it easy to perceive the New Reality into which Jesus beckoned, but many others were afraid. Where spirit is present, it either draws things into its nature to resonate with its qualities and share its joy—or it repels. Christ's teachings meant changes and many were afraid. Many did not allow Our Lord's message to penetrate. Instead, they closed their hearts. Jesus had few real friends during the darkest hours just before the crucifixion. When He cried out on the cross, He symbolized the low point for humanity. Yet He took all that was present and brought the entirety of Himself and His world on through into the Resurrection.

It was a decisive turning point in the history of humankind. It was a breakthrough for the species at last. Here, for the first time since the Fall was a human being attuned to the essences of life, resonating with the breath of the Creator, consciously embodying the Creator's spirit, the Creator's intelligence, the Creator's powerful love. Jesus suffered the worst kind of humiliation and rejection and came on through with flying colors. It proved that there was hope, that further efforts toward restoration and healing were indeed worthwhile. It proved that humankind had not been too badly damaged by the Fall. Humans needed modifications yet. They needed healing and restructuring before they could responsibly house eternal spirit again. But the basic design was still intact.

And on the third day, He rose again.

Despite the seeming failure, despite the apparent power of the materialistic consciousness then holding the world in its iron grip, Jesus proved that one could remain in good spirits, that one could stay happy, that one could express only spirits of God and successfully avoid ill spirits. Jesus pulled on through. He did the will of the Father. Unconquerable life prevailed. Even death itself could not keep Him down.

How many losing teams will not rally when they sense a chance of regaining a victory they had resigned themselves to losing? This is Christ's message! It is a rallying cry for those who still have some spirit, some gumption, some love for the truth, some hope and some courage.

THE HEM OF THE MASTER'S GARMENT

As a child, growing up in the Chicago area, I remember being awed by the fact that every Easter for something like eight or nine consecutive years, it turned out to be a beautiful sunny day. I knew the odds were against this. If you have ever lived in Chicago in March or April, you will know what I mean. Some years, it was cloudy and miserable for weeks, but then sure enough, Easter morning, the sun would be shining warm and friendly and the world would take on a positively brighter outlook.

It makes sense to associate Easter with a fine sunny season. The Resurrection is a joyous celebration of new life. It is the season when what was obscured becomes revealed. Easter celebrates the externalization of the reality of Christ, already whole and complete, finally coming into expression on earth. The Resurrection is spirit fully emerged out of dormancy, beyond the moment of death upon the cross, no longer held down by material restraints. It is life revealing itself once again in a new spring, Christ appearing in the garden.

Jesus was crucified at a place called "the place of the skull." It is through the deviations of the mind that He dies a thousand seeming deaths. However, it is in the place of the heart where He rises once again, rolling away the stony hardness of fear-blocked perceptions, radiating forth in gallant light.

> In the end of the sabbath, as it began to dawn
> toward the first day of the week, came Mary

Magdalene and the other Mary to see the sepulchre.

Matthew 28: 1

Mary was walking in the garden. She had come to pay respects to the tomb where Jesus was buried. She saw what might possibly have meant something wonderful, but then again what might have signified nothing more than grave-robbery. She hoped and longed that the empty tomb might imply resurrection, but everything had been going so wrong lately. Mary's whole world had come apart. She longed to see Christ again. She was frustrated, confused, angry, tired of not knowing what was going on. She stumbled through the garden, half-hoping to find Jesus, but fairly certain that she was just kidding herself. And yet . . . and yet . . . You can almost see her eyes glisten as she determines to "believe, damn it, believe," and go down believing if necessary. She looks up to see a figure standing before her in the garden.

Through her tears Mary could not see clearly. At that moment in her experience she was passing through the veil, she was rolling away a stone that had hardened in her heart. Each of us must pass through a similar experience. At the parameters of human illusion is an emotional veil that one must move through before being able to perceive the resurrected Christ.

Part of the reason for Mary's tears was because she felt that *they* had taken the Lord away. There was a blameworthy *they* in her consciousness at the moment, and until she forgave and released *them*, *they* would be her god, her point of orientation, her chief interest. There was a struggle in her heart between two currents, a divine current represented by her longing for Christ, and a human current that wanted to see *them* get what was coming to them for having crucified Christ and now apparently taken Him away as well.

Mary's emotional backlash was blinding her to what was right in front of her eyes. Her human reactions were based on a false premise. NO ONE CAN TAKE THE LORD AWAY. Jesus' whole life proved that. Circumstances cannot take the

Lord away. Nothing can keep the Lord away from anyone with a passionate interest in meeting Him. When human beings worship false gods, environmental circumstances cause them to be blinded to what is present all around them. They blame the situation for making it impossible to encounter Christ. But this is a cop-out, pure and simple. "Lo, I am with you still, even though you may see me not. And the world sees me not, still I am in you as you abide in me and my word abides in you."

Nothing can take Christ away. The Ascension did not remove the presence of Christ from the earth. It set in motion the process that would one day allow many to take up their historical circumstances and share in Christ's victory over death and illusion. Christ has been on earth ever since the Ascension, working invisibly, gradually allowing His intelligence to dominate the heaven that surrounds the earth.

It is somewhat inaccurate to say that Christ is coming again, for in truth He has never left. He is coming to fallen awareness again. He is coming into power and influence on earth again. But Christ has been here right along. No one can take the Lord away. He is eternally present. Even on Golgotha, in the darkest hour, He was still in charge of affairs. Some may have rejected the gentle teacher of Nazareth, but they understood the earthquake that followed on the heels of the crucifixion. They understood the darkness, the trembling, and the rent in the temple veil.

Mary's veil was also rent as she wandered crying through the garden looking for the Lord. Through her tears she greeted the figure before her. He appeared so healthy, so at ease, so full of life, so at home. She supposed he was the gardener.

> 'Woman,' the figure asked, 'why weepest thou?
> Whom seekest thou?'
>
> 'Sir,' she replied, 'if thou has borne him hence,
> tell me where thou has laid him and I will take
> him away.'
>
> John 20: 15

At this juncture, Mary, like many of us today, was still

looking at things backwards. It is not a dead Christ that we take away to the closet of our belief systems. It is the living, vibrant, radiant Christ who takes us. It is we who step into Christ's reality, not Christ whom we awkwardly try to fit into our own.

Historical Christianity has worshipped an image of a dead Christ. Only an image of a dead Christ will ever fit into a fallen human world, for our human world is fundamentally altered when we open it and ourselves to Christ's living presence. Where there is conscious awareness of the risen Christ, everything is changed, all phenomena are drawn into harmony with His creative love. For all her good intentions, Mary was not open to receiving a resurrected Christ when she first encountered Him in the garden. This is why she did not recognize Him. She was expecting a dead Christ to fit into her world.

The single word, "Mary," broke the spell.

When Mary heard Jesus speak her name, she was reminded of her true nature. The bulk of her experience had not been as a tearful creature. The word, "Mary," called her back to her senses. "Of course, of course!" She began to see. "How obvious. Why didn't I see it before? I didn't want a dead Christ anyway. I wanted a living Christ." But as Mary rushed to embrace Jesus, a curious and symbolic command interrupts her.

"Touch me not," Jesus advises.

If Mary had touched Jesus at this point, the current would have likely killed her. It would have destroyed the circuits of her body-temple. As much as Mary loved Jesus, she did not have any comprehension—indeed she had no way of even beginning to suspect—*how much Christ loved.* The power of Christ's love coming to focus in the resurrected body of Jesus at that moment was for all creatures great and small. Christ's love was for all men and all women throughout all time, into eternity. Mary needed to move into that kind of love. Like all of us, she had to learn how to thoroughly fulfill her human loves, loving her neighbors as herself. Then she might begin to approach the hem of the Master's garment.

Until then, she was not capable of embracing Christ *fully*. She had to first move through the Beatitudinal healing process, developing the spirits, the nature and the temperaments of Christ.

Each human body, mind and heart needs to be tempered little by little, at each stage increasing its capacity to love. It is an incremental process, not necessarily long, but vital and impossible to by-pass. During the stages of this process, one is not imperfect or incomplete. The process itself, when welcomed, brings perfection. Every stage is perfect in the cycles of purification, provided the individual involved is fully open to the healing. Those who pick up their cross and follow Christ have only to accept where they are as their starting point. They might be aware of all kinds of potential, but Christ *is here now*. He is only interested in the potential that can reasonably be invoked *now*. He is not interested in what might be, what will be, or what could have been, but in the best one can do with one's immediate here and now situation.

The young carpenter looks up at his father, "I think I've got all I need, Dad. These scraps are plenty. I can make some neat stuff with this. Thanks." As the boy's skills improve, the father gives him better materials to work with. The boy grows in his craft, and one day he works with the same materials as his father. This was the way for Jesus and it is the way for each one of us. God wants to see how creatively we handle our affairs. If God likes our work, he may give us some larger commission by and by, but not until we have demonstrated our ability to work well with what is at hand.

Though the basic impulse was right, Mary could not fling herself at Christ. That was not the pathway to Christ's temperament. That was not the way to develop her capacity to love. " 'Touch me not,' Jesus commanded, 'for I am not yet ascended unto my Father; but go to my brethren, and say unto them, I ascend unto my Father, and your Father; and to my God and *your* God.' " John 20: 17

Later that day, the risen Christ appeared in a house where the doors were shut, breaking in on the remnants of a group of disciples who were huddled together in fear for their lives.

There is no reason why Christ could not have walked through the very walls. Perhaps He did.

However, my own feeling is that this particular group of disciples was much like Mary had been in the garden. They were afraid, confused, perhaps angry. They were not open to seeing Christ *as one of them,* as a pilgrim on the road, as just another man walking in their midst. They were still looking for the great miracle worker, which of course Christ was as well, but these disciples needed to understand Christ now in another role. They needed to become acquainted with a more personal and immediate facet of Christ's nature.

I have a feeling Jesus slipped up on these disciples, not to impress them with His ability to walk through walls (that was not like Him), but to point out that from here on in, it was a whole new ball game. These new Christians were to begin seeing *themselves* in the identity of Christ. They were to let His spirit shine forth from within each one of them. The experience of the miracle worker, the healer, was now to be theirs as well.

Christ's opening words, "Peace be unto you," set the tone of the new resurrected experience. "As my Father hath sent me, even so send I you." This was the declaration of a new age.

> When he had said this, Jesus breathed on those present and said, Receive ye the Holy Ghost . . .
>
> John 20: 22

A FOURTH LIKE UNTO THE SON OF GOD

In tracing the thread of Christ's impact from His resurrection through to our present era, it becomes obvious that somewhere along the way, something was lost.

SOMEWHERE BETWEEN DAMASCUS AND CONSTANTINOPLE, THE FIRST FLOWERING OF THE HOLY SPIRIT FADED INTO DOGMA AND TRADITION.

I mean no offense to any particular sect or denomination in alluding to this, and I do not mean to imply that the Christian traditions of the past two millennia have not been an improvement upon the ignorance that preceded them. However, since about 300 A.D., the activism of the Holy Spirit has been conspicuous by its absence.

Notice how the human race recapitulates the experience of Jesus: Jesus taught on earth for three years. Early Christianity flowered for three centuries. Jesus spent three days in the tomb and then rose again in glory. Humankind sleeps for a while in a tomb of materialistic illusion and today begins to encounter an unexpected awakening in its midst.

Those of our contemporaries who, like Mary crying in the garden, are looking for an image of Christ, the Christ they expect, will likely remain oblivious until the last moment. They are likely to miss the central phenomenon of all history. Like Mary, they may even encounter Christ face to face and not recognize Him because He did not appear in the form they were anticipating—and subtly demanding. I trust that there are few readers of this book remaining in that category.

I would guess that most of us have begun to recognize the

significance of these times. If you are like me, you long to embrace the reality of Christ that has so long been absent from our human world. But the command at this juncture is to not touch the Lord—not yet.

In the New Heaven our proximity to Christ is determined by our ability to love. Though there is no rigid or fixed hierarchy in Christ, at any given moment some are naturally closer to the core of His being than others. Each one is welcome to approach Christ as closely *as his or her capacity to love will permit.* Those who long to apprehend their Creator more intimately have only to develop their ability to love.

How much of God's love are we willing to accept?

Christ's love is the core of terrestrial animation. It is the fire bringing this earth to life, the electricity behind the scenes. Current is a good thing, but too much current can destroy. You do not plug a 120 volt drill into 220 current. God does not want to burn out circuits. He knows His love is intense.

If the transformative energies of love were to intensify too quickly, things would actually begin to ignite. Our physical conduits would burn up because they had not undergone the incremental tempering of Resurrection. Each and every situation in which we find ourselves, whether adverse or enjoyable, is designed to help us increase our ability to accommodate love.

There is a story in the Book of Daniel that provides insight into this process. It is the story of three friends of Daniel: Shadrach, Meshach, and Abednego. The Bible often uses metaphors this way.

Who are your three closest, most personal friends? Hopefully, they are your body, your mind and your heart. If your body, mind and heart are your friends, then they take care of you, and you take care of them. You are the spirit that governs them wisely, a good friend with a bit of an overview. Such was the case with Daniel and his friends.

As the story goes, King Nebuchadnezzar had a great idol set up on the plain of Dura. He demanded that everyone bow down and worship it. He had oriented to something that looked good. He had established a landmark that he hoped would provide a central reference point for navigation in the land of Babylon. It was conspicuous on the plain of Dura, the level of durability. He demanded that everyone in his kingdom worship it, be guided by it, structure their lives around it.

Those who followed Nebuchadnezzar's dubious advice attempted to create lives based upon material possessions. They tried to build security on the sandy beaches of time. With nothing to work with but sand, their god became durability. The permanence of material wealth was their measure of value. They fashioned images of the earth. This was all they understood.

Daniel's three friends understood a great deal more. They saw the transient and unstable values of contemporary society. They were not interested. The three of them were acquainted with Daniel. They symbolize the body, mind and heart that have frequent exchange with the spirit within. They knew better. They were not influenced by prevalent consumer values. I am sure Daniel's three friends did their best to appreciate the occasional validity that would somewhat randomly emerge from Nebuchadnezzar's morass, *but they had their own values.*

Shadrach, Meshach and Abednego had known some healthy experience under the direction of their inner spirits. They were acquainted with the spirit of the living God. There was no way they could bow down and worship this nonentity that Nebuchadnezzar had set up in the plain. When they came to the plain, as they did frequently to do business, Shadrach, Meshach and Abednego would more often than not forget the idol was even there. For a time Nebuchadnezzar tried to ignore this. But after a while he began to feel threatened. You see, Nebuchadnezzar was not *absolutely* sure himself that this economic idol was all that trustworthy. He harbored a slight fear that Shadrach, Meshach and Abednego's continued casualness and disregard for it might corrupt the consumer values that he foolishly thought his kingdom needed to prosper.

Then was Nebuchadnezzar full of fury, and the
form of his visage was changed against

> Shadrach, Meshach, and Abednego: therefore
> he spake, and commanded that they should
> heat the furnace one seven times more than it
> was wont to be heated. And he commanded
> the most mighty men that were in his army to
> bind Shadrach, Meshach, and Abednego, and
> to cast them into the burning fiery furnace.
>
> Daniel 3: 19-20

Little did Nebuchadnezzar know that he was creating the very conditions that would facilitate the transmutation of Daniel's friends. The fires he thought he had created to destroy were actually the fires of unrecognized love intensifying and coming to focus through his own unconscious cooperation.

Now a very interesting thing occurs here. What do Daniel's three friends (symbolizing his body, mind and heart) do before they go into the fire? They put on pants and hats and coats and other garments. This is pertinent symbolism. It is not *just us* in whom Christ is interested, but in all of that which has attached itself to us. Christ is interested in all the earth that has been drawn into our creative field. As we enter the fires of transformation, our tools of expression enter along with us.

> Then these men, (Shadrach, Meshach and
> Abednego) were bound in their coats, their
> hosen, and their hats, and their other garments
> and were cast into the midst of the burning
> fiery furnace.
>
> Daniel 3: 21

Nebuchadnezzar watched from a safe distance. He could see the furnace's awesome heat. What was this? What was he seeing? The guards had no sooner thrown Shadrach, Meshach and Abednego into the fire when the guards themselves burst into flames. Well, he might have expected as much. He had told them to make it hot. One gets the impression, however, that any momentary sigh of satisfaction from old Neb must have been cut short.

> Then Nebuchadnezzar the King was aston-
> ished, and rose up in haste and spake, and said
> unto his counsellors, Did not we cast three men
> bound into the midst of the fire? They an-
> swered and said unto the King, true O king.
> He answered and said Lo, I see *four* men loose,
> walking in the midst of the fire, and they have
> no hurt; and the form of the fourth is like the
> son of God.

Daniel 3: 24-25

When body, mind and heart are open to the experience of
fully receiving God's love, His love is gentle. Only the bonds
are burned. Only the ropes that had tied back our three
friends, imposing their limitations, are consumed.

> Then Nebuchadnezzar came near to the mouth
> of the burning fiery furnace and spake, and
> said, Shadrach, Meshach and Abednego, ye
> servants of the most high God, come forth, and
> come hither. Then Shadrach, Meshach and
> Abednego, came forth of the midst of the fire.
> And the princes, govenors, and captains and
> the king's counsellors, being gathered
> together, saw these men, upon whose bodies
> the fire had no power, nor was an hair of their
> head singed, neither were their coats changed,
> nor the smell of fire had passed on them.

Daniel 3: 26-27

All of the substance that these individuals carried,
everything that was in identification with them, came through
the fire transformed, it was all included in the raw material
that had been refined. All of the useful ideas, concepts and
notions of the human intellect, all of the innocent, creative af-
fections of the human heart, all of the balanced and healthy
needs of the physical body, all of this is included in the experience of Resurrection. However, the most significant result
of Shadrach, Meshach and Abednego's fiery transformation

was the appearance of the fourth, like unto the Son of God in their midst. Their trust and faith enabled Christ to appear among them.

> Where two or three *(body, mind and/or heart)*
> are gathered together in my name, there am I
> in the midst of them.
>
> Matthew 18: 20

We see nothing in this metaphorical tale of further tribulation. Neither do we find Shadrach, Meshach and Abednego staying in the fire until they are purified according to some arbitrary standard of perfection. No, their very willingness to open themselves to love *was* perfection.

Every moment is not a moment of testing, but when the pinch comes, the true followers of Christ do not hesitate or falter. They are willing to step right into the fiery furnace if necessary. Such confrontation is rarely dramatic. It may occur in the privacy of one's innermost thoughts as one contemplates some lifestyle decision. It may involve the refusal to compromise one's conscience in the course of earning a living. It may just as well occur in a thousand small decisions of daily life as in some great crisis.

The fires of transformation come when we are ready. There is never any need to seek them. We learn to flow with adversity as well as with abundance, in joy, not overjoyed, nor in sorrow dejected. We know what matters. We appreciate Nebuchadnezzar and all the things in his kingdom. We ourselves do business on the plain of Dura, but we would never, even for a moment, consider chasing after material goods or basing decisions on "imagined needs and wants." Though the idols on our plain of Dura may speak in contemporary logic through sophisticated electronic circuitry, they are fundamentally no different from what they have always been.

As we are willing to walk into the fires of self-confrontation if necessary, rather than compromise our integrity in any way, shape or form, that very sentiment assures us of one like unto the Son of God as a friend and companion. And when Christ is present, when God's awareness is guiding our interaction, things do work out. Even Shadrach, Meshach and Abednego's adventure came to a happy conclusion.

> Then Nebuchadnezzar spake, and said, Blessed be the God of Shadrach, Meshach and Abednego, who hath sent his angel, and delivered his servants that trusted in him . . . there is no other God that can deliver after this sort. Then the king promoted Shadrach, Meshach and Abednego, in the province of Babylon.
>
> Daniel 3: 28-30

A COMMUNICABLE EASE

Christ's Resurrection must have been contagious. I get the impression upon reading an account of the events that followed the rolling back of the stone, that virtually everyone Christ met experienced a mini-version of his or her own Resurrection while in the Lord's presence. None were left unchanged. Mary's willingness to stop crying and to look Christ in the eye was similar, I am sure, to the experience of Daniel's friends in the fire. One does not have to be perfect or worthy or ready to face the Lord, only willing and trusting, approaching in perfect faith, and all is done according to promise.

The disciples behind closed doors suddenly saw how utterly ridiculous their fears had been. They were soon going to the other extreme, preaching from the housetops. Even the military commander that the risen Christ touched in passing on the road to Damascus was converted in Christ's presence to become the dynamic apostle Paul. Let's face it, the Resurrection was and is—what shall we call it? A communicable ease?

It is wonderful to live at a time when so many people are beginning to catch the current of the Resurrection experience. It is not difficult to see how it will become the wave of the future, the new way, the only way, the stone, once rejected, the cornerstone of all.

Whether we say something *is happening* or whether we say something *is about to happen* is a moot point. Obviously the Resurrection is going to intensify and reach a collective climax, affecting every creature on the face of the earth. Though that day is not quite yet, the fires of transformation are nevertheless still accessible, available and waiting. Those who voluntarily choose to cooperate with this great process will be spared the tribulations of those upon whom it comes unaware.

Is there a willingness to step trustingly beyond the familiar into the unknown of divine function? The fallen have nothing to lose. Only the bonds are burned, only that which is dishonest is destroyed. Only that which has sought to cheat man of his destiny, which has sought to deny the reality of woman, only that which allows Christ to be crucified in ignorance and disorder, that is all that is threatened, that is all that is burned, that is all that is consumed in the love of the Creator for his human children—nothing more. Is there anything here that interests you? Anything here that you care to defend?

The reality of Christ's approaching Resurrection through collective human consciousness is so profound, so powerful, so contagious that it is *retroactive*. Even though there is a climactic point some years ahead when there will be a shift at the very center of collective human consciousness, the personal experience of the Resurrection is available here and now. During these times of judgment and separation, it is increasingly easy to step into the process of Resurrection. Already it waits for men and women of faith, integrity and courage. Christ's word is, "Take up your cross. Accept yourself and your situation. Accept my life. And follow me."

One gets the impression that there is something to do.

QUICKENING OF SPIRIT

During the Dark Ages, what passed for Christianity was impotent; it was missing something sacred at its core. Without the presence of the Living Christ, the teachings of Jesus were often taken backwards. Many during that age could not help but see God in perpetual conflict with Satan: the forces of light eternally battling the forces of darkness, matter ever seeking to draw humans down, the earth, something to be resisted by those who sought the straight and narrow.

The earth, its nature and tendencies, are not the enemies of spirit. The earth is Christ's partner in love, a graceful, gaseous-blue, oceanic world floating through His awareness. The respective influences of Christ and the earth are good, meant to guide us in the areas of ourselves that correspond to them.

It is good to see the truth; to serve God while in human form is not to deny the earth. It is to share Christ's love for this world and assist in drawing forth her potential. Our historical abuse of the earth, greatly escalated by the industrial era, will not end until our conscious orientation is returned once again to spirit. When our relationship with God is correct, the earth is fulfilled. The earth longs for a polarity reversal in human consciousness just as much as Christ.

The moment we restore our trust in God, everything around us begins to be drawn into the ascending spiral of creative love. Like a whirlwind calling up the dust of a prairie, Christ comes to the earth, His love drawing all who choose into new configurations in a new heaven. What the awakening conscious mind begins to see is beyond anything the sleeping mind had imagined.

It is good to wake up after a bad dream. We have all had nightmares that seemed vivid and real in the darkness. In the morning light, they have no meaning. We wake. We laugh. We forget them and we move on. I am naturally interested in the resolution of world events, but I refuse to worry about them. I have already seen the patterns of their resolution take shape in heaven. There are variables, of course, but the fundamental healing of humanity, the Resurrection of Christ, is already complete.

Events on earth are all leading toward Resurrection. All terrestrial processes, creatures and conditions will pass through the veil of transition, the fire of transformation. All will be either blessed and healed through God's love, or consumed in the fire of love's most elementary manifestation. It does no good to become emotionally involved in issues outside the realm of our responsibility. I do not know about your home and neighborhood, but the fire intensifying in these parts is a fire of blessing and purification. It is consciously directed. And it knows what it is doing.

As the angel rolled away the stone from the mouth of the tomb, that the Resurrected Christ might come forth in glory, so the angel of potential within each one of us must roll back the stone that has barricaded the entrance to our hearts. The reality of who we are is not to be forever confined. The hour has come. Our centuries in the sarcophagus are complete. We have no more time for the ancient hardness of heart that has blocked our perception of God. Unwavering, we approach the stone until it dissolves in a thousand particles of blinding light. It is time to re-emerge into the garden of consciousness. Nearly twenty centuries ago, the apostle Paul wrote movingly of this experience.

> There are also celestial bodies, and bodies
> terrestrial: but the glory of the celestial is one,
> and the glory of the terrestrial is another.
> There is one glory of the sun, and another glory
> of the moon, and another glory of the stars: for

one star differeth from another star in glory. So also is the resurrection of the dead. It is sown in corruption: it is raised in incorruption: It is sown in dishonour; it is raised in glory: it is sown in weakness; it is raised in power: It is sown a natural body; it is raised a spiritual body. There is a natural body, and there is a spiritual body. And so it is written, The first man, Adam was made a living soul; the last Adam was made a quickening spirit. Howbeit that was not first which is spiritual, but that which is natural; and afterward that which is spiritual. The first man is of the earth, earthy: the second man is the Lord from heaven. As is the earthy, such are they also that are earthy: and as is the heavenly, such are they also that are heavenly. And as we have borne the image of the earthy, we shall also bear the image of the heavenly. Now this I say, brethren, that flesh and blood cannot inherit the kingdom of God; neither doth corruption inherit incorruption. Behold, I shew you a mystery; We shall not all sleep, but we shall all be changed, In a moment, in the twinkling of an eye, at the last trump: for the trumpet shall sound, and the dead shall be raised incorruptible, and we shall be changed. For this corruptible must put on incorruption, and this mortal must put on immortality. So when this corruptible shall have put on incorruption, and this mortal shall have put on immortality, then shall be brought to pass the saying that is written, Death is swallowed up in victory. O death, where is thy sting? O grave, where is thy victory? The sting of death is sin; and the strength of sin is the law. But thanks be to God, which giveth us the victory through our Lord Jesus Christ. Therefore, my beloved brethren, be ye stedfast,

unmoveable, always abounding in the work of
the Lord, forasmuch as ye know that your
labour is not in vain in the Lord.

I Corinthians 15: 40-58

Every being feels a quickening of spirit, an intensification at
the approach of Christ. A quickening of welcome and love will
heal and create. A quickening of fear will destroy. The first
man, of which fallen humans are aware, is of the earth. His
chaotic and incongruent short-sightedness has created the first
heaven and the first earth that must pass away. The second
man is the Lord from heaven. His is the spiritual nature that
the first man is designed to honor, respect and obey. If we
worry about the things of the earth, our hearts will be
vulnerable to the fluctuations of the world around us; but if we
remember our first love, and love first the ways of spirit, we
perceive reality.

"AS IT WAS IN THE BEGINNING . . ."

As we feel the Holy Spirit waking up within us, what once appeared dead now stirs and comes to life. We find ourselves sitting up in the darkness of the tomb. The grave clothes are upon us. We begin to remove them; the concepts, the beliefs, the images, the ideas, the paradigms new and old. They have been woven so tightly around us, we were hardly able to move. They have obscured our life. As we step out of their decaying fabric, we don the celestial bodies that God has prepared for us. Bodies of light, resembling our present physical bodies as glowing light bulbs resemble bulbs without current. And the current, the new current, is so refreshing! Our burden is light—wonderful *illuminating* light! We are purified and rejuvenated. The truth dissolves unreality in its path. The stone that once imprisoned us becomes transparent in the radiance of the Lord from Heaven.

The stone was an illusion, the lie commonly agreed upon. We once sustained it through fear and ignorance. But we have glimpsed the garden beyond the stone. We can no longer agree to the myh of the stone's solidity. We begin to gather with others who feel the same. We agree in spirit. We perceive the risen Christ.

Something is changing deep within. A shift is initiated at the center of things. Do you feel the forgotten hopes of something stirring deep in your soul? We knew it when we were young. We watch. We keep our lamps burning. We do not allow the fires of our love to diminish. We sense His presence among us, yea even in our own hearts. We hear His

Word. We are educated. We step into the garden of a New Earth, under a New Heaven, a living member of the body of Christ. The New Heaven is here for those with eyes to see. When we first step under the unfamiliar stars in its sky, we are aware of something far beyond the historical level of human experience.

It is ingenious the way Christ has engineered our healing. What a wonderful mechanism the apparent succession of generations has been. Christ was not willing that any should perish, at least not without the best possible chance. The breadth and scope of His behind-the-scenes historical engineering is phenomenal, almost unbelievable.

Every effort possible is being made to convey the Way of eternal life to incarnate humans. The teachings of Jesus (as recorded in the King James Bible) provide a survival manual for fallen spirit. Christ has gone to great lengths to educate us through every available avenue. Though we have been unconscious of His Presence, He has contrived and designed, juggled and re-engineered to keep as many of us as possible in His Presence until His comprehensive plan of salvation had time to work out.

What do you suppose Jesus was talking about when He said with such emphasis, "Verily I say unto you, *this generation* shall not pass, till all these things be fulfilled?" Matthew 24: 34

What generation was Christ referring to? To whom was He speaking at the time?

He was surrounded by those who loved, respected and trusted Him, surrounded by His disciples. That moment actually occurred: Jesus Christ, incarnate in a physical body, speaking to His disciples. It was a real historical moment. It symbolized and brought to precise focus another moment, a moment of supreme significance, an eternal moment *that is the source* of all we know or have ever known.

There is an eternal spiritual moment pulsing steadily and consistently behind the ever-shifting scenes of history. In it, Christ is surrounded by his disciples, dressed in biological robes, incarnate in an ever-changing human family. We are part of that moment. We are Christ's generation. We are generated, brought into being, by His Presence.

When Christ comes within a certain range of the earth, the substance of earth is drawn into Christ time and Christ space. Matter reflecting His vision and purpose is animated and suspended in His love. This is Christ's generation; His love is the energy at its core; His truth is spinning its designs.

Christ lives at the core of all terrestrial life. You and I know life and consciousness to the degree that we are in Christ's Presence. Since we are alive physically, we are already in Christ's *physical* Presence. Christ is waiting for us to look up. We are his favorites, the survivors. The Middle Ages have come and gone. We are still around.

Each one now alive has had a continuity of spirit from the moment Christ said, "I am the resurrection, and the life: he that believeth in me, *though he were dead,* yet shall he live: And whosoever liveth and believeth in me *shall never die.*" John 11: 25-26

We are Christ's generation.

We are the only generation that ever was or ever will be.

Christ has kept us close to Him. He has kept us young. He has kept us close to the source of life in Him. We are spirits surrounding the Presence of Him who is our own innermost eternal self. Each succeeding life wave has allowed Christ to draw His fallen children to greater levels of intelligence, hoping that when the end time came, they would be perceptive enough to recognize the signs of His return. Many of Christ's parables spoke of the nature of His return to human consciousness. Those who believed in Him would be alive when it occurred.

The apparent succession of generations has kept the Fall from becoming fatal. Each new wave of life rippling out from Christ contains children whose eyes sparkle just a wee bit more and whose spirits are just a bit harder to keep down. Each succeeding generation is lighter and more buoyant than the last. Our children are part of Christ's generation, just as we are. But we are fooling ourselves if we think we can pass this cup on to our children.

We are the ones.

We are the spirits alive in Christ's generation. Are we dreaming a foolish vision of a fallen world?

Until we awaken, until we discover *how* Christ is apprehended, until we look up and *perceive* Him and restore Him as the central factor in our conscious lives, we are but half-incarnate creatures, subject to as much chance as intention, as much chaos as direction.

Are you willing to break through any remaining illusions? Are you willing to enter the baptism of fire? There is no better time. Today is the day of decision for this generation. Christ's spirit has been, and is now, bubbling beneath every human illusion. It is your spirit, our spirit, the spirit of the family of eternal god-beings to which we belong.

Our prototypes incarnated initially in Eden, but as a species, as a global human family, we have yet to fully enter the earth. We are the generation who will incarnate for the first time.

The "I" *that is Christ* is dotted by every "we" in humanity.

TERRA CHRISTA

I once viewed a time-lapse motion picture depicting the growth of a flower. In the space of a few seconds, I watched something break through the soil, grow tall, blossom, release its seed, wither, die and fall away again into the soil. The first frame showed only an empty patch of dirt. The flower came and went. The last frame again showed only an empty patch of dirt.

I wonder what it would be like to watch a time-lapse motion picture depicting the life of an oak tree. Would the acorn crack in two and release a tiny shoot toward the sun? Would the slow centuries of golden maturity elapse in a few seconds? Would one see a blurry succession of owls, woodpeckers, squirrels, and insects helping the magnificent tree's return to the soil?

Suppose we were somehow able to take a time-lapse movie of the growth of an entire forest. What would it reveal? What would it resemble waving in the winds of continual change that shape and mold our mother planet?

What if we could watch a time-lapse movie showing the entire lifespan of the earth? Would we witness the face of the planet bubbling and boiling in the warm rays of the sun? Would we see biological life as a sort of slow-combustion, gradually releasing the potential of the earth, the structural principles of universal truth boiling over the fires of eternal love? Would we see mountains form and re-form with the fluidity of clouds?

We would certainly be sure to slow down the film and zoom

in to have a closer look at those curious humanoid creatures that would suddenly appear almost everywhere. Just what would a time-lapse movie of the appearance and future of *Homo sapiens* reveal? Are we a flower, to fall back into the soil? Or might such a time-lapse glimpse of humanity's future show the earth releasing something to the stars as a dandelion releases her seed to the wind?

We have come a long way—spirits in a material world. The cycle will not end without fulfillment, without giving birth to another cycle. Infinite universal potentialities will continue to unfold. We have Christ's promise that some of us will participate with Him in that unfoldment.

During these last days when the final sorting is intensifying, we are aware of the need for healing in our human affairs. We share Christ's longing that all men and all women of all races, nations and creeds might join us in peace, joy and well-being. We remain in the currents of God's love where truth, both universal and immediate, is always available. We remain in the Way, the Truth and the Life. This ensures our maximum contribution toward healing as this age draws to a close.

We appreciate the many forms of understanding that flow through our lives as the Holy Spirit is welcomed, but there will always be newer, fresher, truer packages than the linguistically-framed concepts of today. Languages themselves evolve as channels of perception deepen and expand. New realms of understanding open up like the seasons that grace the forest or the succession of perennials in a formal garden. At what season is the garden perfect? What stage in the growth of a flower or a child is incomplete?

Living perfection is written upon the fluid screen of time with the graceful pen of change, motion, surprise and delight. We allow all these things to flow through us. And it continues. The earth rolls to face the sun. We turn to face God, to love God with all our hearts, with all our souls, with all our minds. The blessings rain gently from a New Heaven. The sun shines upon a New Order of the Ages.

We rise up in union with our deepest nature. One in Christ. The power comes. The magic enters. The current flows. The eye of the human family is single, Terra Christa, one spirit, one song, one purpose, one life, one earth.

I rejoice for you as you no doubt do for me. We rejoice for the presence of every one with open heart and honest intention. In love with one another as the Creator loves us, it is done. In a moment. In the twinkling of an eye. All is transformed. The earth is healed. A universal species emerges from the womb. A joyful open-ended age of conscious creation commences. All are immersed in the enjoyment, exploration and development of space.

ACKNOWLEDGEMENTS

I would like to thank the many individuals who have helped to make this book possible. There are so many special spirits who have contributed so very much that I will ask them all to forgive me if I single out only one, my wife, Sherry, who is responsible for these pages every bit as much as I am. To her and to the many others, I am grateful.

There are several groups whose influence has contributed positively to this book and to whom I am particularly thankful. I would like to thank and acknowledge the Roman Catholics who struggled for years to educate me, the Baptists who taught me how to sing, the Methodists who provided me (indirectly) with the most centered wife in the world, the Society of Emissaries who did their best to make me respectable—but failed—and the Amish who taught me a trade and the joys of spirit-filled work.

I would also like to thank Giovanni Guareschi, wherever he may be, for authoring four little books about a lovable Italian priest named Don Camillo that have afforded me much entertainment when I needed to relax after long hours at the typewriter. I suppose in addition I should extend my appreciation to the Human Family whose long and tragic record of mistakes has provided so many valuable learning experiences, but one really must draw the line somewhere. I know for a fact that there have been many others throughout my life who have offered me a welcome influence. As their contributions are reflected in these pages, my gratitude extends to them all.

BIBLIOGRAPHY

Asimov, Isaac. *The Human Brain.* New York: Mentor, 1963.

Augustine, Saint. *Confessions of Saint Augustine.* Translated by Edward B. Pusey. New York: Macmillan Co., 1961.

Bentov, Itzhak. *Stalking the Wild Pendulum.* London, England: Wildwood House LTD., 1978.

Bohm, David. *Wholeness and the Implicate Order.* London, England: Routledge & Kegan Paul, 1980.

Boone, Allen J. *Kinship With All Life.* New York: Harper & Row, 1954.

Campolo, Tony. *You Can Make The Difference.* Waco, TX: Word Book Publishers, 1984.

Carey, Ken. *Vision.* Kansas City, MO: Uni-Sun, 1985.

Chesterton, G. K. *Orthodoxy.* New York: Doubleday, 1973.

Chesterton, G. K. *St. Francis of Assisi.* New York: Doubleday, 1957.

Cousins, Norman. *Anatomy of an Illness.* New York: Bantam Book, 1981.

Dobson, Dr. James. *Emotions, Can You Trust Them?* Ventura, CA: Regal Books, 1980.

Frankel, Viktor E. *Man's Search for Meaning.* New York: Pocket Books, 1963.

Glass, Bill. *Expect To Win.* Waco, TX: Word Book Publishers, 1981.

Graham, Billy. *Angels: God's Secret Agents.* New York: Pocket Books, 1976.

Graham, Billy. *Approaching Hoofbeats: The Four Horsemen of the Apocalypse.* Waco, TX: Word Book Publishers, 1984.

Graham, Billy. *The Holy Spirit.* Waco, TX: Word Book Publishers, 1978.

Hubbard, Barbara Marx. *The Evolutionary Journey.* San Francisco, CA: Evolutionary Press, 1982.

Jones, Marc Edmund. *The Sabian Manual: A Ritual For Living.* Stanwood, WA: Sabian Publishing Society, 1957.

Jones, Marc Edmund. *The Sabian Book: Letters of Insight.* Stanwood, WA: Sabian Publishing Society, 1973.

Keller, Philip. *A Shepherd Looks at the Good Shepherd and His Sheep.* Grand Rapids, MI: Zondervan Publishing House, 1979.

Keyes, Ken Jr. *The Hundredth Monkey.* St. Mary's, KY: Vision Books, 1981.

Krieger, Dolores, PH.D., R.N. *The Therapeutic Touch.* Englewood Cliffs, NJ: Prentice-Hall, Inc., 1979.

Kubler-Ross, Elisabeth. *On Death and Dying.* New York: Macmillan, 1970.

Lahay, Tim. *Study the Bible for Yourself.* Eugene, OR: Harvest House Publishers, 1976.

Leonard, George. *The Silent Pulse.* New York: E.P. Dutton, 1978.

Lewis, C. S. *A Mind Awake: An Anthology.* Edited by Clyde Staples Kilby. New York & London: Harcourt Brace Jovanovich, 1980.

Lewis, C. S. *The Joyful Christian.* Riverside, NJ: Macmillan Publishing Company, Inc., 1977.

Lewis, C. S. *Mere Christianity.* Riverside, NJ: Macmillan Publishing Company, Inc., 1978.

Lewis, C. S. *Miracles.* New York: Macmillan, 1960.

Lewis, C. S. *The Screwtape Letters.* Riverside, NJ: Macmillan Publishing Co., Inc. 1967.

Lindsey, Hal. *The Terminal Generation.* Old Tappen, NJ: Spire Books, 1976.

Marshall, Peter. *The Light and the Glory.* Old Tappen, NJ: Manuel, David.
Power Books, 1981.

McDonnell, Thomas P. *A Thomas Merton Reader.* New York, NY: Harcourt, Brace & World, Inc., 1938.

Meeker, Lloyd A. *The Divine Design.* Loveland, CO: Emissaries of Divine Light, 1979.

Meier, Paul D. and Minirth, Frank B. *Happiness is a Choice-A Manual on the Symptoms, Causes and Cures of Depression.* Grand Rapids, MI: Baker Book House, 1978.

Naisbitt, John. *Megatrends.* New York: Warner Books, 1984.

O'Connor, Elizabeth. *Eighth Day of Creation - Discovering Your Gifts and Using Them.* Waco, TX: Word Book Publishers, 1971.

Pearce, Joseph C. *Magical Child.* New York: Bantam Books, 1980.

Raphael. *The Starseed Transmissions.* Kansas City, MO: Uni-Sun, 1982.

Robertson, Pat and Slosser, Bob. *The Secret Kingdom.* New York: Bantam Books, 1982.

Russell, Peter. *The Awakening Earth.* London, England: Routledge and Kegan Paul, 1982.

Ryan, Travis. *The Wellness Workbook.* Berkeley, CA: Ten Speed Press, 1981.

Sanford, Agnes. *Creation Waits.* Plainfield, NJ: Logos International, 1978.

Schuller, Robert. *Tough Times Never Last, but Tough People Do.* Nashville, TN: Nelson, 1983.

Schuller, Robert. *Tough-Minded Faith for Tenderhearted People.* Nashville, TN: Nelson, 1979.

Seamands, David A. *Healing for Damaged Emotions.* Wheaton, IL: Victor Books, 1981.

Shelldrake, Rupert. *A New Science of Life.* Los Angeles, CA: J. P. Tarcher, Inc., 1981.

Stanley, Charles F. *Handle With Prayer.* Wheaton, IL: Victor Books, 1982.

Swindoll, Charles W. *Dropping Your Guard - The Value of Open Relationships.* Waco, TX: Word Book Publishers, 1983.

Swindoll, Charles W. *Growing Strong in the Seasons of Life.* Portland, OR: Multnomah Press, 1983.

Swindoll, Charles W. *Standing Out.* Portland, OR: Multnomah Press, 1983.

Taylor, Jack R. *The Hallelujah Factor.* Nashville, TN: Broadman Press, 1983.

Teilhard de Chardin, Pierre. *The Future of Man.* New York: Harper & Row, 1969.

Thompson, William Irwin. *Passages About Earth.* New York: Harper & Row, 1973.

Watson, Lyall. *Lifetide.* London, England: Hodder & Stoughton Ltd., 1980.

Wilkerson, David. *Jesus Person Pocket Promise Book.* Glendale, CA: Regal Books, 1979.

Also by the author of **TERRA CHRISTA**, UNI*SUN is proud to make available the following books:

THE STARSEED TRANSMISSIONS — AN EXTRATERRES-TRIAL REPORT, by Ken Carey

Already in its 4th printing and rapidly becoming a classic, **The Starseed Transmissions** are regarded by many as the clearest and most articulate expression of the "extra-terrestrial message" that is presently being broadcast to the earth. Thousands of telepathic individuals around the world are picking up this message in various forms, but nowhere has it been recorded with such power and breath-taking economy of expression. Beginning with an interpre-tation of human presence on earth that strikes a hauntingly familiar chord, **Starseed** moves on to provide what may well be the most coherent overview of human history to appear in this generation. Just reading **The Starseed Transmissions** is itself a step into the unknown, the rhythmic language of-ten triggering the very states of consciousness from which it comes. Enjoy a new way of understanding, an experience, a gift from beyond the stars. Discover **Starseed . . .** and remember!

95 pages, perfect bound: $6.95

NOTES TO MY CHILDREN — A SIMPLIFIED METAPHYSICS, by KEN CAREY

"I have always thought," Carey states in the Introduction, "that upon incarnation, upon becoming conscious in a physical body, our children were due some kind of report— something that would let them know what kind of planet they had surfaced on, what the conditions were in this par-ticular age, what the basic game plan was and what strategies they might realistically adopt. This book is based on talks that I had with my own children attempting to provide them with precisely this information. My parables are not meant to be taken literally; they are designed to awaken and nourish the child spirit in all."

Richly illustrated, **Notes To My Children** covers the same basic territory as **The Starseed Transmissions**, but in a manner suitable for children from 9 to 99. Humorously referred to by the author as *"a toddlers first comprehensive overview of life on this planet,"* **Notes** is an enjoyable journey through fact & fantasy, full of short stories that children feel good after hearing—entertaining analogies and tales designed to convey, not dogma, which children tend to forget anyway, but spirit, spirit which will be with them long after the particulars of each tale are forgotten.

172 pages, perfect bound, illustrated: $8.95

VISION, by KEN CAREY

"**Starseed** and **Vision** form one single seamless concept. They are, I feel, the modern restating of much of the Book of Revelation, but more excitingly, **Vision** takes off into fresh, previously uncharted territory, unveiling the destiny of Mankind as a single organic unit, with a future beyond this solar system. The message is handled with such deftness, gentleness and love, single sentences make dozens of modern books on the average bookstore shelf obsolete. I am humbled by its beauty, power, clarity, accuracy—by the Truth which shines from every page. **Vision** is a most important book for our Age."

— Ron Ross, former owner/editor of New Age Press

A message from the Creator, from the Eternal Spirit at the

Source of all Life, **Vision** is a powerful sequel to **The Starseed Transmissions**, a book that could revolutionize our understanding of what it means to be human . . .

93 pages, perfect bound: $6.95

RETURN OF THE BIRD TRIBES, by Ken Carey

In this exciting new channeled narrative, best-selling author Ken Carey reveals the story of the Bird Tribes: ancient, angelic inhabitants of the North American Continent who continue to shape its destiny. These gentle spirits offer a new perspective on the birth and life of Jesus Christ, and plot a course of harmonic unity for the red, white, yellow and black races into the next era of history — one without fear. Like all of Ken Carey's remarkable books, **Return of the Bird Tribes** is full of hope, love, inspiration and joy.

"A stunning, shimmering, joyfull experience. Congratulations on helping us all to share a new dimension of being."
—Wayne Dyer, author of **Gifts From Eykis**

"A very well written book that captures the Native American feeling. I enjoyed reading it immensely."
—Sun Bear, author of **The Medicine Wheel**

256 pages, $11.95 in soft cover, or $16.95 in hard cover

OTHER BOOKS AND PRODUCTS

We at UNI ★ SUN are happy and proud to publish books and offer products that make a real contribution to the global spiritual awakening that has already begun on this planet. The above books are a sampling of what we have available. Please write for our free catalog.

UNI ★ SUN
P.O. BOX 25421
KANSAS CITY, MISSOURI 64119
U.S.A.

WORKSHOPS AND SEMINARS

For information on workshops and seminars by Ken and Sherry Carey write:

Starseed Seminars
Star Route, Box 70
Mountain View, Missouri 65548